# HEAVEN
*and*
# NATURE
# SING

HANNAH ANDERSON

# HEAVEN

*and*

# NATURE

# SING

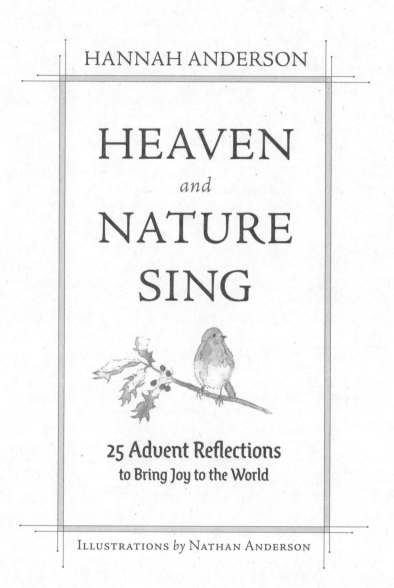

## 25 Advent Reflections
### to Bring Joy to the World

ILLUSTRATIONS *by* NATHAN ANDERSON

B&H
PUBLISHING
NASHVILLE, TENNESSEE

978-1-0877-7678-1

Published by B&H Publishing Group
Nashville, Tennessee

Dewey Decimal Classification: 242.33
Subject Heading: ADVENT—MEDITATIONS / CHRISTMAS
/ JESUS CHRIST—NATIVITY

Author is represented by Wolgemuth & Associates.

Cover design and illustration by Nathan Anderson.
Author photo by Mary Wall.
Background texture Lukasz Szwaj/Shutterstock.

1 2 3 4 5 6 • 26 25 24 23 22

For Naomi Ruth Detandt (1970–2021), who honored Christmas in her heart and tried to keep it all the year long.

# Contents

———— JOY ————

———— PEACE ————

# Author's Note

This book contains twenty-five essays designed to carry you through the weeks before Christmas. Commonly known as Advent, these weeks mark the start of the church year and have historically been a time for reflection, fasting, and prayer focused on the second coming of Jesus, not necessarily his first. In fact, in some church traditions, Christmas decorations and celebrations are held off until Christmas Day in much the same way that Lent does not end until Easter morning.

Today, however, Advent is more often observed as a kind of "soft opening" for Christmas. Most of us know the season because of Advent calendars that help us count down the days with little treats or activities. This approach to Advent leads us to Christmas, not by deprivation but by invitation, giving us a sneak peek of what's coming.

With this book, I hope to split the difference, giving you a chance to prepare your heart for Christmas by considering both why Jesus came to earth in the first place and why we so desperately long for his return. I want to offer you hope—not by ignoring the brokenness but by looking it squarely in the face, knowing that your Redeemer has and will come. And I want to tell that story through the lens of the natural world, to consider how not just we, but *all of creation*, waits for our Creator King.

I was originally inspired in this direction by Isaac Watts's 1719 hymn "Joy to the World." Although we know it as a Christmas carol, it was written as an Advent hymn because it looks forward to the day when Jesus will reign and the world will finally be at peace. Of course, it's impossible to separate the first and second comings. The Son who came is the Son who will come, and our need of him today is no less than it's ever been or ever will be.

So, how should you read this book?

If you did not grow up with traditional rhythms of Advent, you may find such habits difficult to keep consistently. Because of this, let me invite you to read these reflections with the month of December as a guide. Simply begin on December 1 and reward yourself with a chocolate with each reading. The twenty-five meditations will carry you through to Christmas Day.

If, however, you prefer to follow the rhythms of the liturgical calendar, you may read each section (marked by the headings Hope, Faith, Joy, and Peace) in coordination with the four weeks of Advent. This should deliver you to Christmas Day in an orderly fashion as well.

But perhaps your approach to the days before Christmas is more like mine. If so, feel free to begin this book with the best of intentions, get busy with holiday preparations, lose it among the gift wrap, find it two weeks later, and binge several readings in one sitting to catch up. This, too, will deliver you to Christmas, as I have never known the day to wait until I was ready for it.

In any case, may the grace that first brought the Son of God to earth carry you through these next few weeks. May you discover afresh his kindness and goodness. May you long for his kingdom to come, and may you find yourself singing his praise with all creation.

# Wintering

Here, where I live in the mountains of southwest Virginia, December marks the beginning of winter. Night gathers quickly, with a deep darkness settling in by the time we settle around the table. The ground, that only a few months earlier burst with life, lies dormant under a chill that never seems to lift. From the warmth of my kitchen, I look out the window to see my once-lush garden encrusted with ice, full of thick, heavy clods of earth, and littered with the remnants of cornstalk and pumpkin vine that twist up among the table scraps.

The red raspberry canes stand bare, imitating dead sticks quite believably. The strawberry plot has been rifled for the last bits of fruit, and all that remains are dark, decaying leaves. The herbs have been cut back to their slumbering roots. And on particularly cold mornings, the asparagus I left to bolt is encased in frost, its fern-like leaves crystallized so that each segment is clearly visible.

Closer to the house, ornamental beds of lily, hosta, and peony hide their delicate parts deep within the earth. The grape vine that climbed the arbor in summer and whose clusters hung over us while we ate and drank in the sun is bare, stripped and cut back in expectation of next season. The peach trees raise bony limbs against a perpetual gray sky. And across the way, the fields lay in patchwork browns, punctuated occasionally by tussocks of rusty broom sedge. I can see straight through the thicket of trees now, their naked trunks and leafless branches as thin as wisps of hair on an aging head.

In December, it's hard to believe that the earth ever brought forth life or that it ever will again.

But winter also brings the holidays, and so we do our best to be merry despite the landscape around us. We wrap bare limbs and sleeping bushes in brightly colored lights, the miracle of electricity compensating for their previous buds and blooms. We stoke fires to make up for the sun's absence and fuel them with seasoned wood, disproportionately pleased by our ability to salvage light and heat from death. The wintering birds will get an extra helping of seed, and eventually, we'll cut a tree and drag it into the front room. We'll scour the woods for bits of green—Virginia pine, holly, eastern hemlock, and if we're lucky, mistletoe—and drape them along the mantle, windowsills, doorways, and banisters.

I wonder, though, if we're really scouring for hope, searching for those small, steady promises that reassure us that the gathering night and the present interlude is only temporary. I wonder if, like the earth itself, we're waiting, holding our breath in anticipation, longing to believe that something more is happening, that something more is coming. I wonder if we're all just waiting for God to show up.

In Romans 8, the apostle Paul writes that "the sufferings of this present time are not worth comparing with the glory that is going to be revealed to us"—that no matter what we're currently going through, no matter the heartbreak, no matter the confusion, no matter the grief or loss, God's goodness and glory await us. That deep, under the surface, out of sight, he is at work. That he always has been, and he always will be. To prove this, Paul turns our attention to the natural world:

> For the creation eagerly waits with antici-
> pation for God's sons to be revealed. For
> the creation was subjected to futility—not

willingly, but because of him who subjected it—in the hope that the creation itself will also be set free from the bondage to decay into the glorious freedom of God's children.[1]

It's a strange thing to think of the earth this way—as having a will or having to wait or even having the ability to hope for redemption. Even stranger that the earth would be our partner in hope, longing for freedom and life and glory as much as we do.

But when I look out my window in December, when I see how much the world around me has changed in only a few weeks, when I see its lifeless stillness, I believe it. And when I remember what Genesis tells me—that I was made from that same ice-encrusted earth, that a curse of futility hangs over us both, that "from dust you were taken and to dust you will return"[2]—I know it in my bones.

Yes, the heavens declare the glory of God, and the earth shows forth his handiwork just as Psalm 19 says they do. And yes, when I gaze into the inky blackness of a December night and see a thousand points of light, I can almost hear a chorus of praise. But when I see a mountaintop cut bare for the minerals beneath or I remember the whirlwinds that level neighborhoods or I watch on the news as fires consume home and forest alike, I hear something else. I hear a groaning that mirrors my own. I hear a longing and a pain that cries out for redemption.

And I find in nature an unexpected ally in the work of hope.

So in this season, as we celebrate the Creator who took on flesh and came to his creation, we do so in solidarity with an entire cosmos. Here in these moments of Advent and Nativity, heaven and nature sing, teaching a truth we cannot know without the witness of both. It is a story of bodies and skies and beasts and trees—all waiting for the glory that will be revealed when the Son of God comes to his own. It is a story of longing and incarnation, of the earth receiving a flesh-and-blood Redeemer, first as a Baby and one day forever as its King.

I want to invite you into this story afresh. To consider the Christmas narrative from a slightly different perspective—to think of all the ways Jesus's coming changed and will change the world. To truly believe that in response to the Savior's reign, "fields and floods/Rocks, hills and plains/Repeat the sounding joy."[3]

For as much as we are part of this same creation, made from the very ground that lies beneath our feet, it is our story as well. So that even as our mortal bodies waste away and the ground continues to groan, we take hope. The One who loved the world came to it. And from this love, he will redeem it until both the earth and those made from it slip from the bondage of decay to eternal glory. Until the children of God are revealed.

Because just as Jesus came to this world through birth, the Scripture promises that we enter the heavenly kingdom through rebirth and that one day the earth itself will give birth—not just to another season, but to our resurrected bodies.

And now you know why heaven and nature sing. Now you know why those of us who dwell in the dust must awake and sing along with them, why a chorus of "joy to the world" is on our lips. Here in this season, with its quiet, pervasive witness to both life and death, when we're most fully aware of the darkness can we become most fully aware of the light. Here our cries for deliverance become songs of praise. And here, between what is and what will be, I am most convinced of the glory that must come.

Because here, where Advent turns to Nativity, creation itself teaches us to hope in our Creator, infant King.

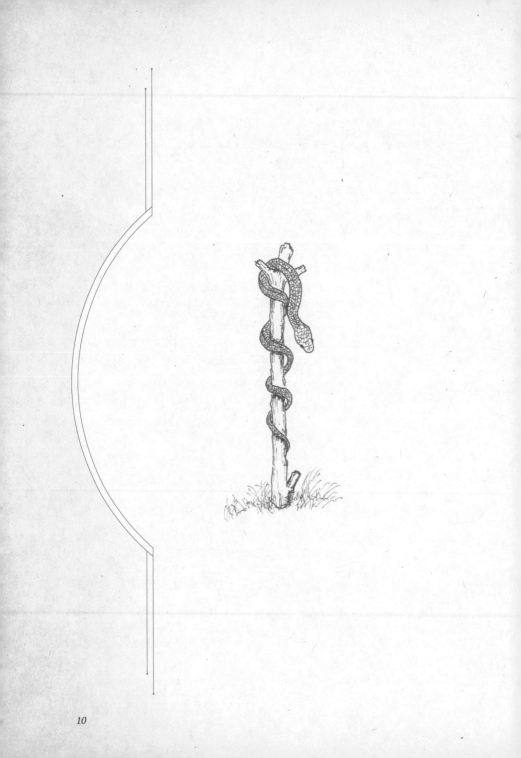

# 2

# The Serpent

"Kill it again, Charles! Kill it again!"

I'd heard the punch line a dozen times, but it never failed to send me into a fit of giggles. That my grandma, the strongest, bravest woman I knew, would be the source of it made it even funnier.

She'd grown up ·in the mountains during the Great Depression, the middle child of ten. Her people were farmers who understood the goodness of hard work, laughter, and family, so once a year, we'd make our way back to their hills for a reunion where the siblings swapped memories and told tales on one another. I remember passels of cousins by varying degrees, games of softball, an outhouse, a creek, and tables full of food—potato salad, ham, and butterscotch pie.

But my favorite time for stories was curled up in my grandma's bed on the nights I was allowed to stay over. Our days together were for work—cleaning, blackberry picking, and gardening—but the nights were for storytelling. She'd dress me in layers and socks and tuck me in under piles of blankets. Sweating, I'd throw them off, but she'd put them right back on, determined that I wouldn't be cold.

Then in the darkness, I'd whisper, "Grandma, tell me about the time . . ."

I had a whole repertoire of stories to choose from: the time she'd overturned the churn and spilled the family's cream for the week or how she walked three miles to high school in good weather and boarded in town in bad. But one of my favorite stories was when she and her older brothers were out making hay under a blazing summer sun.

She'd been assigned to the top of the wagon, and as her brothers threw up pitchforks of hay, she'd stamp them down to make room for more. The system was working fine until a tremendous black snake came flying through the air straight at her—an unfortunate hitchhiker on someone's fork of hay. As quickly as it had come up, she sent it back down, where her brother stabbed it. But satisfied with nothing less than the reptile's eternal damnation, she screamed, "Kill it again, Charles! Kill it again!"

In all fairness to the snake, seeing one in a hay field isn't uncommon, and most are entirely harmless. There's the black racer—long, shiny, darting here and there; the northern ring-necked with its yellow collar; and the eastern garter, a striped snake that apparently to someone, somewhere, once resembled the aforementioned accessory. You will occasionally spot more harmful snakes, the kind that send a shiver up your spine and have earned the aversion we carry against the species as a whole. Timber rattlers make their home in wooded areas, blending into the underbrush, while their neighbor the copperhead prefers more open habitats like overgrown fields, dilapidated barns, and rock ledges.

When you encounter a snake, however, the best thing to do is nothing. Even a venomous snake would rather move along than bite you. So catch your breath, calm your heart, and watch it for a few seconds before it glides out of sight. If you do, you'll see one of the most unexpected, and unnerving, spectacles in the animal kingdom.

Limbless, a snake propels itself in waves, writhing and slithering along the ground. To climb, it will coil around a tree or pole, scrunching and creeping upward. To burrow, it relies on "rectilinear locomotion," a unique coordination of scale and muscle movements that allow it to push its body forward in a straight line. Surprisingly, this uncanny way of getting around is the first specific animal phenomenon recorded in Scripture. And perhaps even more surprisingly, the snake is the first to receive the promise of Christmas.

According to Genesis, after God made the man and woman, he placed them in a garden which they shared with the animals. For a while, everything was good and beautiful and exactly as God planned; but a twist was coming, a twist in the form a winding, coiling, curling reptile. One day a snake shows up, and with subtle, hissing words, convinces them to do the one thing God had forbidden: to eat from the tree of the knowledge of good and evil. Immediately, a curse descends; the man and woman are banished from the garden; and nothing is the same again.

For its part in the deceit, God sentences the snake to its unique movement:

> You are cursed more than any livestock
> and more than any wild animal.
> You will move on your belly
> and eat dust all the days of your life.

But then he promises this:

> I will put hostility between you and the
>     woman,
> and between your offspring and her
>     offspring.
> He will strike your head,
> and you will strike his heel.[1]

Theologians call this passage the *protevanglium*, or the first announcement of the good news, because it foreshadows the birth of the One who will undo the serpent's deceit along with its lethal aftermath. Eve's hope—our hope—was that this coming Promised Son would crush the serpent and all it represents, even as he suffers in the process.

But here's something curious: the news of a Redeemer wasn't given to Eve, not directly at least. It was given to the snake. And it was given in the form of a warning: judgment is coming. The power you hold over the earth will one day be taken from you. So for the snake, Christmas is far from good news. Or is it?

Of course, the snake of Genesis 3 is not simply a snake, not like the ring-necked and garter snakes in my backyard. Revelation 12:9 speaks of an "ancient serpent, who is called the devil and Satan, the one who deceives the whole world." And elsewhere in Scripture, snakes represent sin and our own bent toward falsehood. Romans 3, for example, says

> There is no one who does what is good,
> not even one.
> Their throat is an open grave;
> they deceive with their tongues.
> Vipers' venom is under their lips.[2]

In this sense, we are also the hissing, deceitful ones. We, too, creep and crawl along the earthly plane. We, too, face certain judgment.

But here's something even more unexpected than the fact that Christmas was first announced to a reptile. In John 3, Jesus likens his redemptive work to a miracle that occurred centuries earlier when God healed the Israelites of poisonous snakebites by having them look to a bronze serpent on a pole. "Just as Moses lifted up the snake in the wilderness," Jesus says, "so the Son of Man must be lifted up, so that everyone who believes in him may have eternal life. For God loved the world in this way: He gave his one and only Son, so that everyone who believes in him will not perish but have eternal life."[3]

And just like that, those who once followed the snake into damnation, now proclaim the grace of Christ in salvation. Those cursed by their own disobedience are now blessed by the obedience of another. I wonder about this. I wonder how the snake—so long associated with sin and death—could be associated with Christmas. I wonder until I remember the heart of the Creator for his creation. The God who knows every sparrow that falls, who numbers the stars, who holds the seas in his hand—would this same God let his creation be taken from him? Would he so easily give up what he has created and called "good"?

No. This is a God who redeems. This is a God who restores—both for those who have suffered under the deceit of sin and those who have deceived others. Because one day, evil will be crushed under the heel of the Promised Son, and his blessings will flow "far as the curse is found."[4]

And when he does, the snake that was once a sign of sin's dominion will become a sign of our complete and final redemption. In Isaiah 11:8–9, the prophet tells us of the day when the Promised Son will finally and fully reign over his creation. In that day,

> an infant will play beside the cobra's pit,
> and a toddler will put his hand into a snake's
>     den.
> They will not harm or destroy each other
> on my entire holy mountain.

The hope of the snake is our hope. We, who with poison on our lips have deceived and been deceived, to us, the promise is given: a Savior has come, and a Savior will come. And when he is lifted up, all who look to him will find life—everlasting and eternal.

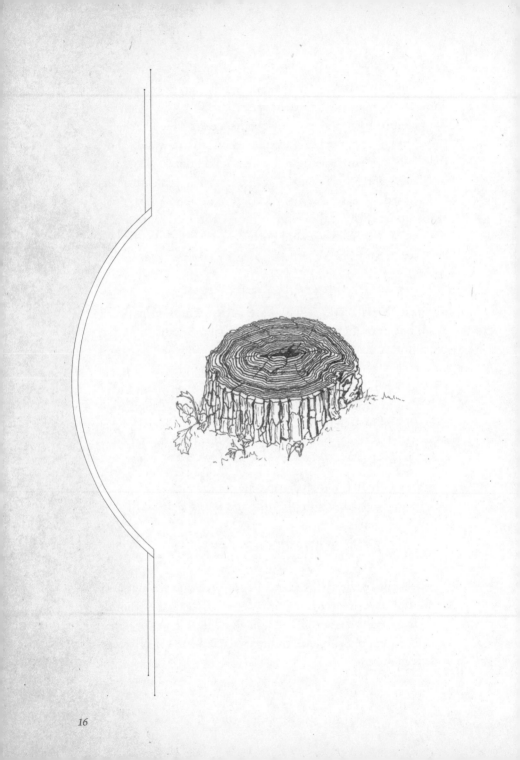

# 3

# Family Tree

Some time last year, my husband, Nathan, returned from his parents' house in the mountains with a cardboard mailing tube. It had obviously been repurposed, with the words 1 MAP PALESTINE N.T. TIMES crossed out. Next to them, his dad's mother had written: "Two genealogy charts—somewhat finished, to be researched." Inside, we found the aforementioned charts, one of his grandmother's ancestry ("somewhat finished") and one of this grandfather's ("to be researched").

On Nathan's side, Grammy is the keeper of the family history, and over the last few decades, she's devoted significant time to tracking down marriage certificates, land transfers, and newspaper clippings. Because of her, we know that Nathan's great-great-grandfather emigrated from Denmark and wrote for his bride to follow. We know that he could apply to the Sons of the Revolution. And perhaps most interestingly (at least to my children), we know rumors of a long-lost estate somewhere in England that was the inheritance of a certain third son of a certain lord who escaped a "political disturbance" by coming to the colonies.

So when I unrolled the charts, I was surprised to find large sections of them blank.

Unlike a family tree that branches to show the offspring of a particular couple, these were ancestral fan charts. They were laid out in a semicircle, documenting the ancestors of one specific person by marking preceding generations with concentric rings—much the same way the rings of a tree mark its age. But on these charts, almost every line past five or six generations (roughly two hundred years) was blank. Despite decades of research, it was patently obvious how much we didn't know. How much we would never know.

Our family's dilemma is not uncommon in modern society, particularly for those of us whose ancestors moved (or were forcibly *removed*) during the age of migration and colonization. For my family, life in the New World meant leaving behind particular ethnic traditions and national loyalties to be eventually integrated into the racial and national categories of American society. So while I treasure family stories and I can make some vague claim to being "Swiss German" or "Scotch-Irish," I really don't know much about my heritage beyond a couple hundred years.

The fragility of generational identity hit home for me on a recent family trip to Northern California. We'd stopped at several groves of coastal redwoods, those towering old-growth hardwoods whose size is matched only by their age. Every so often, we'd come across a giant cross-section cut from a fallen tree. With its rings exposed, you could literally see the centuries, even millennia, as each concentric circle marked a growing season. And to make sure we got the point, many of these giant slabs also had metal plates marking historic events that occurred during the tree's lifetime. With the outermost edge being closest to the present, the rings created a time line as you moved toward the center: World War II, the Emancipation Proclamation, the Boston Tea Party, the invention of the printing press, the *Magna Carta*, and so on and so forth, all the way to the birth of Jesus himself.

As fascinating as it was to view these living records of history, it was also incredibly humbling, especially when I realized that my knowledge of my own generational rings would have reached only a few inches from the circumference.

But what does this have to do with Christmas?

In Genesis 3, God promised that the "seed of a woman" would crush the serpent's head and turn back the curse. In other words, God promised to work generationally. And while Genesis 4 hints that Eve may have thought her firstborn was the Promised Son, time would prove redemption to be much more expansive and much more enduring than anyone could imagine.

When you read the records of Jesus's ancestry in Matthew 1 and Luke 3, you're reading more than a list of names. You're counting the rings of a family tree that represents the out-working of God's plan of redemption. A plan that reaches back through the nation of Israel, through the covenants with David, Abraham, and Noah, all the way to the garden.

But like our personal family histories, the story of redemption is far from seamless. Because over the years of waiting, many generations lost hope. In the waiting, in the longing, they gave up. They turned from God and his promise and turned to idols to live for the present moment. They abandoned God's ways and forgot the coming Son.

As a result, they suffered judgment. Faithful prophets went silent. The temple was desecrated, and the people scattered. Their homeland became prey for foreign invaders until, in the words of Isaiah 6:11, the "cities lie in ruins without inhabitants, houses are without people, the land is ruined and desolate."

Describing this work of judgment, Isaiah likens it to a tree cut down: "Look, the Lord GOD of Armies will chop off the branches with terrifying power, and the tall trees will be cut down, the high trees felled."[1] So if the genealogies in Matthew and Luke are rings of the tree of redemption, it's a tree that has been cut down. It's the story of generations displaced and a land decimated. Without a family, there is no Promised Son. And without a Promised Son, there is no redemption. It's a story that seems hopeless.

Almost.

Because while Isaiah prophesied that generations would be cut down like a tree, he also prophesied that a remnant would remain and that "the holy seed is the stump."[2] Despite all the loss, all the devastation, God had not abandoned his promise. And while we may be unfaithful to it, he is not. One day

> a shoot will grow from the stump of Jesse,
> and a branch from his roots will bear fruit.
> The Spirit of the LORD will rest on him. . . .
> On that day the root of Jesse will stand as a
> banner for the peoples. The nations will look
> to him for guidance, and his resting place will
> be glorious.[3]

The story of Christmas is this: the tree is not dead. A shoot will live and grow. And grow and grow and grow.

Until eventually others are grafted into the root—strangers and foreigners and all those who never thought they'd know family again, those who never dared to hope that life would run through them. Until one day, this tree grows so large and so old and so majestic that its branches fill the earth.

When I think about this, how the work of God takes time, even generations, it quiets me. And when I think about how close it all seemingly came to being undone, it humbles me. You and I are links in the chain of generations, called to steward the fragile hope we've received. The seventy or eighty years given to us on this earth pale in light of those who have come before us and those who will follow after. But more than this, our individual lives pale when compared to the God who sustains our hope.

So whether his work happens over the course of a thousand years or one day, whether it is given to us to play a prominent role in it or simply to stand as a faithful witness to the promise, we will wait on him. And we will wait in hope.

The tree is not dead. The quiet, steady work that came before us will continue on after us. The quiet, steady work we do today—even if it's as simple as celebrating the Promised Son during this season—will echo through the years. Until one day, we find ourselves gathered together with all those who have hoped in him, with all who have found him faithful from generation to generation.

# 4

# Anointed One

Y ou know, Mom," the voice echoed through the dimly
lit sanctuary, bouncing off the stone floor and mul-
lioned glass, "theoretically speaking, holy water is a limitless
resource. As long as a solution is more than 50 percent holy
water, the whole thing becomes sanctified. It's brilliant. If you
do it right, you'll *never* run out."

This lesson in sacramental chemistry came shortly before
midnight and shortly after the conclusion of a Christmas Eve
service at a friend's church. Navigating our way out of the
sanctuary, we had just passed an elaborate baptismal font, one
presumably filled with water that was at least 51 percent holy.
Like Nathan and me, our children have spent their formative
years in small Baptist churches, a fact that ensures their inter-
est in more ancient ones. But as it is for so many of us raised
in low-church traditions, we only know sacramental practice
in theory. So when we visit more liturgical services, there's still
a novelty to it all—including the holy water.

Not that we Baptists don't have our own liturgies, especially
around the holidays. We can fill the weeks before Christmas
with just as much meaning as the next tradition. Here's how
I've experienced it: sometime in late October, the countdown
to Christmas begins with a scramble to organize the children's
play. We drag out sets, hand out parts, sort through costumes,
and sew ears and tails. Simultaneously, the adult choir begins
practicing their cantata, including the work wooing its delin-
quent members back "just for Christmas." The Sunday after

Thanksgiving, we'll start singing carols. Tom will offer his annual rendition of "Star of Bethlehem," and Rhonda will show up in her collection of holiday sweatshirts, one for each Sunday in Advent.

The tree will go up, and someone will order the fruit baskets for caroling. But the real fun comes with the church-wide Christmas dinner, an affair packed with ham biscuits, Jell-O salads, sweet potato casseroles, red velvet cake, and homemade Christmas cookies. After which, the deacons will distribute brown paper sacks filled with old-fashioned candy, jelly slices, peanut brittle, coconut balls, and the largest navel orange you'll see all year. (I wouldn't believe such things still existed either if I hadn't seen them myself.)

Having experienced both high- and low-church worship, I'm fascinated by tradition and how we determine the boundaries of sacred practice. The question becomes even more pressing when I consider the witness of the natural world. After all, if Elizabeth Barrett Browning is right, if "Earth's crammed with heaven/And every common bush afire with God,"[1] how do you differentiate certain days, spaces, and times as sacred? How do we set aside this one and not another? How exactly do you ensure the purity of holy water?

The paradox of the sacred and mundane sits at the heart of the Christmas story, and we're first introduced to it in Luke 1:5–6 when we meet Zechariah, a priest married to a woman named Elizabeth. Both are "righteous in God's sight, living without blame according to all the commands and requirements of the Lord." They are also elderly and childless.

As the story begins, Zechariah is serving in the temple sanctuary, burning incense before the Lord. Known as the "holy place," the sanctuary held the golden lampstand, the table of shewbread, and the altar of incense. The book of Exodus describes this incense as being made from equal parts of the spices stacte, onycha, galbanum, and frankincense, a recipe that was to be used for no other purpose and was regarded as "holy—belonging to the LORD."[2]

So there beside the altar, Zechariah is entering into ancient, sacred rhythms that stretch back to the time of Moses. But they are not unbroken rhythms because the holy place in which he now stands once lay in ruin, desecrated and defiled. Repeatedly ransacked by foreign invaders, Solomon's temple fell in 586 BC, and while Ezra rebuilt it roughly seventy years later, it was eventually defiled, too. In 167 BC, in a graphic show of force, Antiochus IV Epiphanies erected a statue of Zeus in this second temple and used the sacred altars to sacrifice pigs.

It's been said that hope has two beautiful daughters: anger and courage.[3] Anger at the way things are and courage to see that they don't stay the same. So seeing the temple defiled in this way, a hope-filled priest named Matthias initiated a revolt that was eventually completed by his son Judah the Hammer. Within a few years, they'd regained control of the temple and began reestablishing worship.

But here's the thing about holy places: you can't just start worshipping again. The priests, the temple, and all its vessels had to be re-sanctified. Under the Law, this included a process of anointing them with holy oil. But like the incense Zechariah burned, this anointing oil was made from earthy, common things. It consisted primarily of olive oil—perhaps the most mundane substance in the ancient Near Eastern world, used for everything from food to medicine to hygiene to light.

So I can't help but wonder, how can something so mundane sanctify? Shouldn't holiness come from rare and special things? How can the ingredients for holy oil be so common? And then I remember the words of Paul in 1 Timothy 4:4–5: "For everything created by God is good, and nothing is to be rejected if it is received with thanksgiving, since it is sanctified [or made holy] by the word of God and by prayer."

The oil itself is not holy. It is *made* holy. It becomes holy when it is set apart by and for a holy God.

But there was another problem. Having begun the process of rededicating the temple, Judah and the other priests find that all the vats of oil set apart for the golden lampstand had also been defiled—all except one. But this cruse only held enough oil for one night, and the lampstand had to burn continuously (or at least long enough for them to make and consecrate more oil). There was simply not enough. After all the years of fighting, all the pain, all the loss, there was nothing to be done. Had their faithfulness been in vain? Was their hope misplaced?

But then God stepped in.

Tradition says that each night the flame was kept alive by a miracle of provision. The oil that should have lasted only one night kept flowing from the jar and lasted eight nights instead—enough time for the priests to press and consecrate more. I wonder if they thought of the widow of Zarapheth on those anxious nights, how God provided her with enough flour and oil to last the whole famine. Or maybe they remembered the mother and her sons who poured oil from pot to pot to pot in an exercise of hope—always ready for it to run out, always finding it enough.

Some scholars suggest that the tree of Isaiah 11—the tree whose shoot will grow from the stump—is an olive tree, both because of its ability to "bear fruit" and because the olive tree sends up shoots around its base. And this makes sense because *Messiah* and *Christ* mean "the anointed one," the One set apart by the pouring of holy olive oil.

But like his ancestor David, who was the least obvious choice to be anointed king, there would be nothing obvious about the Promised Son. According to Isaiah 53:2, "He didn't have an impressive form or majesty that we should look at him, no appearance that we should desire him." The Promised Son would look like any other man. But by coming this way, by coming in the flesh, he would sanctify our flesh, making the world sacred by his presence.

So we should not be surprised that this same Anointed One celebrated the miracle of the provision of oil, going up to the temple for the Festival of Dedication.[4] Nor should we be surprised, that like the common olive crushed to provide that holy oil, he too would be crushed for our holiness—that "he was pierced because of our rebellion, crushed because of our iniquities; punishment for our peace was on him, and we are healed by his wounds."[5]

Today, celebrations of Advent and Christmas overlap with the celebration of Hanukkah or the Festival of Dedication. But just as oil and water are made holy by a holy God, the significance of these days does not lie in the days themselves, but in the One to whom the days are dedicated. In the same way, those of us who follow Jesus are a people set apart, but not because of anything in us. We, like the olive tree, are common. But like the holy oil that comes from the olive, we have been sanctified, made holy by the Holy One.

So like those who waited through those anxious nights so long ago, we put our hope in God's provision; we trust that the One who provided anointing oil also provided the Anointed One. And on the days when you feel too common for God to use, when you find yourself overrun, defiled, and desecrated, rest in this hope: the holiness of God never runs out, and his grace is as limitless as he is.

# 5

# Silence

To my family's great disappointment, living this far north of the equator is still too far south to ensure a white Christmas. In fact, in the ten years I've lived in southwest Virginia, we've only had one. Thankfully, because we at live at a high enough elevation, we do get several good snowfalls a year, just not during the holidays.

Advances in meteorology usually mean we have fair warning of them, the only downside being that these same advances tend to get our hopes up before a storm actually materializes. What you can count on, however, are natural signs that predict precipitation more locally: blue-gray skies that hang heavy above your head, a drop in temperature and barometric pressure, a ring around the moon, and the sudden flurry of animal activity as deer and junco prepare for the coming weather.

And then, when the conditions are right, the snow will begin to fall. Unlike rain or sleet that bounces off roofs and strikes against windows, snow's unique shape and composition mean that it drifts to the earth in an almost unnatural silence. Soon it will cover the grass and pile up along the fence line. The roads will turn from black to white, and if the storm lasts long enough, school will cancel and we'll settle in for a day of rest. Then, as quietly as it began, it will stop, leaving the world covered in white.

But the silence continues somehow. In those first few hours after a snowfall, a hush lies over the landscape. If I didn't know better, I'd think my mind was playing tricks on my ears. As if by covering up the muddy ruts and scattered toys and barren trees, the snow had somehow reduced the sound as well. Has my brain mistaken a visual peace for an auditory one?

My brain is not playing tricks on me, but the truth is less surprising than if it were. Scientifically speaking, it is quieter after a fresh snowfall. A snowflake's six-sided crystalline structure creates small spaces—open pockets, you could say—that absorb sound waves. Because of this unique shape, snow dampens noise much the same way foam panels in a recording studio do. And the more accumulation you have, the greater the effect. In fact, some studies show up to a 60 percent reduction in sound with just a few inches.[1] At least, at first.

As the snow crystals begin to melt, they change shape and lose their buffering properties; and as the cycle of "melt and refreeze" settles in, laying snow becomes dense. A thin crust of ice can develop which actually magnifies sound waves as they bounce off the hardened surface. What once absorbed the sound, giving the world an unexpected experience of calm, now amplifies it.

While it might surprise you, the dynamics of silence and sound are key to understanding the years between the Old Testament and the New Testament. Known by some theologians as "the silent period," the four hundred years after the end of Malachi and before the beginning of the Gospels was marked by the absence of God's voice. Like a fresh snowfall blanketing the landscape, a hush had descended. This doesn't mean God wasn't present or at work during the intertestamental period, but that, in the words of 1 Samuel 3:1, "the word of the LORD was rare and prophetic visions were not widespread." In fact, Jewish theologians mark Malachi as the last prophet God sent to Israel and believe that he has not spoken since.[2]

Interestingly, the book of Malachi actually ends with the promise that God will speak again through a prophet who will be like Elijah in his power, authority, and courage: "Look, I am going to send you the prophet Elijah before the great and terrible day of the LORD comes. And he will turn the hearts of the fathers to their children and the hearts of children to their fathers."[3]

But by the time Zechariah is serving in the temple, it hasn't happened, and the previous four centuries have been marked by suffering, loss, and a pervasive silence. So when Luke picks up the narrative, the questions have also changed. The question isn't simply when will the prophet come, but *will he come at all? And what happens to hope when you can't hear God's voice? What happens to hope when you begin to believe that God can't hear your voice?*

Returning to Luke 1, we find Zechariah standing beside the altar of incense where suddenly, while in the act of offering up prayers, the angel of the Lord appears to him. At first, Zechariah is terrified, but the angel comforts him, reassuring him that he has good news. Zechariah's wife, Elizabeth, although elderly and thought to be barren, is going to conceive a son. This son will be named John and be filled with the Holy Spirit even before he is born. He will be the prophet God promised at the end of Malachi, and his life's work will be to prepare Israel for the coming Promised Son.

But by the time the angel stops speaking, Zechariah has moved from fear to disbelief. And all the waiting, all the wondering, all the doubt surfaces: "How can I know this?" he blurts out. "For I am an old man, and my wife is well along in years."[4]

At this point, the angel identifies himself as Gabriel, the one who stands in the presence of God, and as he continues, you can almost hear the reproof in his words: "I was sent to speak to you and tell you this good news. Now listen. You will become silent and unable to speak until the day these things take place, because you did not believe my words."[5]

As a person whose vocation depends on my words, I can think of nothing more terrifying than losing them. You press your lips together in protest. You raise your soft palate, opening wide to let an objection escape. The tip of your tongue touches your alveolar ridge. Your face muscles contract, and you can feel your vocal cords vibrating. But there is no sound. You have been silenced. Muted and—for all you know—unheard.

But something more than reproof is happening in this moment. And to understand why Zechariah's words are taken from him, you must remember Gabriel's first words to him: "Do not be afraid, Zechariah, because your prayer has been heard."[6]

The irony of Zechariah losing his voice is that he had been using his voice to beg God to intervene. But somewhere along the way, he'd lost hope that God was hearing him. Somewhere along the way, he found himself asking, "If a prayer leaves my lips but God doesn't answer, does it make a sound?"

Zechariah was about to learn that our inability to hear God's words is no measure of his ability to hear ours. Even when he is silent, he hears. He sees. He knows. And even if he works on his own timetable, he still works. So to prove his faithfulness, God takes Zechariah's voice. He takes it as if to say, "I will be faithful to you with or without your prayers. You just stand there and watch. You just watch."

Because when all is said and done, it is God who speaks worlds into existence. It is God whose voice echoes across the void and says, "Let there be light."[7] It is God who fills wombs that stand as silent as space. It is God who answers Hannah's prayers when "her voice could not be heard."[8] It is

God who knows our needs before we express them.[9] It is God who himself intercedes when our words fail—who "helps us in our weakness, because we do not know what to pray for as we should."[10]

And so perhaps God's reproof was not a punishment for Zechariah so much as an invitation to experience his strength in a way that could only happen in weakness. Perhaps God's *"now listen"* was not silencing Zechariah so much as quieting him, quieting him long enough to restore his hope. Because just as the snow's icy crust amplifies sound instead of absorbing it, our prayers ring loudest in our ears when we believe they are unheard.

So God is going to prove that he is a God who hears.

How appropriate then, that when the Father finally speaks, it is to answer a prayer for a child. How appropriate that this child will one day be known as "the Voice" who cries out to prepare the way of the Promised Son. And how appropriate that a story that starts with the silence of God leads to God's greatest Word ever.

Because in just a few short months, the One who existed from the beginning would be born. "Long ago," writes the author of Hebrews, "God spoke to our ancestors by the prophets at different times and in different ways. In these last days, he has spoken to us by his Son."[11]

And so as we wait through our own silent periods, we wait in hope. The One who heard and answered Zechariah is the same One who hears us today. The One who sends snow to quiet the world is the same One who quiets our hearts even when we can't hear him. And the One who restores our hope is the same One who will open our lips to declare his praise when we finally can.

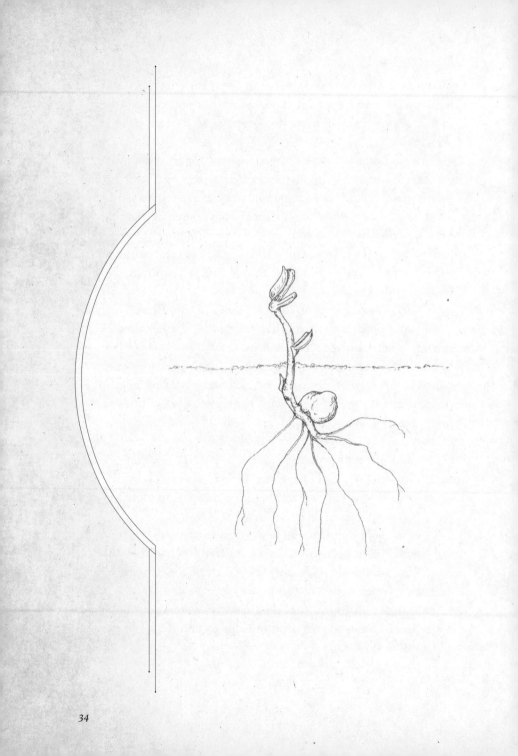

# 6

# Holy Seed

When you hear the word *creation* or *nature*, do you think of your own body? Or do you tend to think about whatever is not human, whatever is out there, apart from you—the trees, mountains, sky, and animals?

If you're like me, you might have to pause a moment before you answer. Theoretically speaking, I know that human bodies are created by God and that he's called them "good" since the beginning. But experientially, there's this gap between my sense of self and the world around me. Like many people in modern society, it often feels as if I'm observing the natural world rather than participating in it.

But the more I learn about how creation praises its Creator and the more I learn about my own place in it, the more I believe that my *body*—not just my will or consciousness—sings a part in that song. In fact, in Psalm 139, David considers his physical body to be one of the clearest expressions of God's power and wisdom, even from its earliest moments:

> For it was you who created my inward parts;
> you knit me together in my mother's womb.
> I will praise you
> because I have been remarkably and
>    wondrously made.
> Your works are wondrous,
> and I know this very well.
> My bones were not hidden from you
> when I was in secret,
> when I was formed in the depths of the
>    earth.[1]

In this season when we celebrate the Promised Son coming in human form—a human *body*—we must not miss how our bodies testify to God's faithfulness. But to do this, you'll have to back up to the beginning, back to the time when God created you in the darkness of your mother's womb. But of course, that's exactly where the story of Jesus's body begins as well.

After Luke introduces us to Zechariah and Elizabeth, he turns our attention to a young woman named Mary who lives in Nazareth. She is a relative of Elizabeth, and like her, she too receives a visit from the angel Gabriel. Unaccustomed to such heavenly visions, Mary is naturally afraid, but Gabriel calms her and tells her she has found favor with God and "will conceive and give birth to a son, and you will name him Jesus."[2]

There's only one problem. While God may be the one who creates human bodies, he uses a process called sexual reproduction to do it. We share this process with many trees, flowers, and animals, and although Mary likely didn't know the details of how it all worked, she knew a human baby needed a father. She was engaged to a man named Joseph, but they were not yet married, and she was a virgin. So she's understandably confused. Gabriel reassures her: "The Holy Spirit will come upon you, and the power of the Most High will overshadow you. Therefore, the holy one to be born will be called the Son of God."[3]

We could explore the significance of this virgin birth at length (as many theologians have), but don't miss the startling reality that the Bible is holding out in front us: the Promised Son was . . . *conceived.*

Just like us, Jesus spent nine months growing inside his mother's womb. Just like us, his physical body went from ovum to zygote to embryo to fetus to newborn. And whatever we might conclude about the uniqueness of his conception or the way this uniqueness plays itself out in his life and ministry, there's something to learn from conception itself.

During a fertile period each month, a woman's ovaries release an egg to be potentially fertilized by a father's sperm. If it is not, the egg exits the body along with the uterine lining during her menstrual cycle. But if the egg is fertilized and conditions are right, a few days after fertilization, it will implant in her uterus—much the same way a seed is planted into the ground—beginning a nine-month process of growth and development.

In this sense conception is a *promise*. When a couple sees a positive pregnancy test or hears a first heartbeat, it is a promise that in a few months' time, they will receive a living child into their family. We call them expectant parents because they are *expecting* the promise to be fulfilled. But even as joy and hope take center stage, loss and grief wait in the shadows. Because at no point is pregnancy or birth assured. In fact, the reproductive process is so vulnerable that many people say a third to one-half of fertilized eggs never attach to the uterine wall, leaving the body without implanting. Of those that do implant, another 10 to 20 percent will be lost to miscarriage, never having the chance to develop. This agonizing, grief-inducing effect of the fall has been women's reality, not just in our time but for ages.

So, when Mary received the announcement of the Promised Son, she did not yet receive the reality of the Promised Son. While the word of the Lord may be sure, it was not yet fulfilled, and between the promise and its fulfillment, between faith and sight, between conception and birth, we find hope.

In this moment, Mary had a choice: she could doubt the angel as Zechariah had, or she could receive the word of God in faith, believing it was true. Only time would prove whether her hope was well placed or not, but in this moment, with the angel standing before her, she chooses to believe. "See, I am the Lord's servant," said Mary. "May it happen to me as you have said."[4]

And once she believes, it changes her. Because once a mother has the hope of a child, she begins to prepare for that child. She changes her diet, she tells her closest friends and family, and she gathers all that she'll need to care for her coming little one. In her hope, she behaves as if the promise is true.

In James 1, Scripture likens our salvation to the process of birth, writing that God the Father "by his own choice, he gave us birth by the word of truth so that we would be a kind of firstfruits of his creatures."[5] Building on the metaphor, James continues: "Therefore, ridding yourselves of all moral filth and the evil that is so prevalent, humbly receive the implanted word, which is able to save your souls. But be doers of the word and not hearers only."[6]

In much the same way a fertilized egg implants in a mother's womb or a seed sprouts from the ground, the word of God begins to take root in our lives, sometimes before we even understand what is happening. An encounter here, a word there, something like trust and hope slowly developing inside of us. But once we do understand what God is doing, once we understand the promise of new life, it changes us. Because just as an expectant mother cares for the life inside her, changing her habits and acting in hope that this child will come, we too must become "doers of the word and not hearers only."

In this way, conception and pregnancy teach us the shape of the Christian life. They teach us how to behave as we wait for our hope to show itself to be true, to walk according to what we've heard and what we expect. Consider what the apostle John writes in his first epistle:

> See what great love the Father has given us
> that we should be called God's children—and
> we are! The reason the world does not know
> us is that it didn't know him. Dear friends,
> we are God's children now, and what we will
> be has not yet been revealed. We know that
> when he appears, we will be like him because
> we will see him as he is. And everyone who
> has this hope in him purifies himself just as
> he is pure.[7]

Like our own bodies that once developed in the secret parts of our mother's womb, our hope develops in small, secret ways, cultivated by the hand of God. And so for us, the question is whether we will receive the promise of God—whether we, with Mary, will say, "I am the Lord's servant. May it be done to me according to your word." And then live as if all the things we say we hope for are actually true, even when they seem improbable or impossible.

Because the reality was that Mary was a virgin. It simply wasn't possible for her to conceive. It wasn't possible for the Promised Son to come from her womb. But as Jesus himself would one day teach, when the disciples questioned how any of us could be saved, "What is impossible with man is possible with God."[8]

And so in this same hope, we live, believing that quiet, small acts of faith will grow into something greater and more life-giving than any of us can imagine. So that when we finally begin to feel those small flutters and kicks, when hope begins to move and dance inside of us, we believe the promise even more. Until one day, hope is finally birthed into the world, and we see the Promised Son with our own eyes.

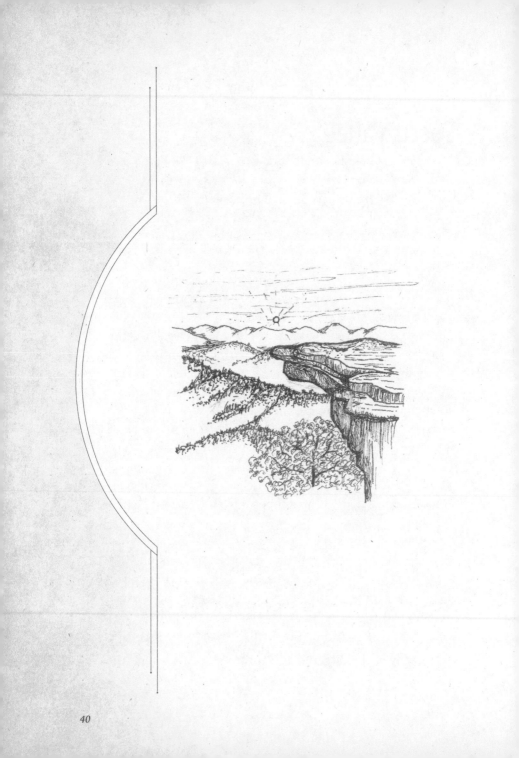

# 7

# Every Valley

When Nathan and I moved back to Virginia, we knew we wanted to put down roots so we decided to buy our first house. Having both grown up in the country and spent the previous eighteen months in the relentless flatlands of Indiana, we were more than ready to nestle into green, rolling hills. Circumstances being what they were, we did most of our house-hunting online, arranging to visit potential properties over the course of a few days.

One house seemed particularly promising. It had the right number of bedrooms, sufficient square footage, and came with several acres. But when we arrived, we realized that while the property did come with the listed land, the plot was almost entirely vertical. The house sat at the bottom of a steep embankment and took up most of the level ground. And because of the way it was positioned, surrounded on so many sides by hills, we wouldn't see the sun until midmorning.

Such positioning is not uncommon here. Hollows (narrow, sheltered valleys surrounded by steep hills) are almost synonymous with mountain life. Their unique shape means that the time between "sunup" and "sundown" is significantly shorter, and people who live in the hollow literally have less light than those further up the mountain or on a plain. We ultimately passed on that property, opting for a smaller piece whose flatness compensated for its size. We can watch the sun rise steadily in the east, and at night when it dips behind the horizon, if a bit earlier than we'd like, our sacrifice is rewarded with breathtaking sunsets and rose-colored hills.

Finding level land on which to build is only one of the challenges that come with life in the mountains. Once off the highways, there are no straight roads and even fewer direct routes anywhere. Running errands will take you up and down hills, along ridges, through valleys, and across streams. But you'll quickly get your bearings because the roads are often named for the surrounding landforms. Robert's Mountain Road runs around the base of Robert's Mountain. Pleasant Valley Road runs between two ridges (and allows you to do the same). Windy Gap Road is exactly as it sounds, but don't expect to take Crockett Gap Road all the way to Hardy's Mill unless you have four-wheel drive and nerves of steel.

Geologists will tell you that these mountains were once part of the same range as the Scottish Highlands and the Atlas Mountains of North Africa. The Pangean Range was itself originally the result of shifting plates and colliding continents that caused the ground to buckle and fold over in a cataclysm of geology. Mountains were thrust to the skies while "the fountains of the great deep"[1] rushed from the earth through the resulting canyons and gorges. And while the Blue Ridge Mountains are no Rockies or Alps, they are our mountains, and I'll never get over how much the land itself shapes life here. Even to something as simple as who gets to see the sun first.

So, when Luke writes that "Mary set out and hurried to a town in the *hill country* of Judah,"[2] he has my full and complete attention.

After Gabriel's visit, Mary goes to her cousin Elizabeth who has also received miraculous news. While the Bible does not say this explicitly, scholars think Zechariah and Elizabeth may have lived in Hebron, one of the towns given to the priests as an inheritance and a city of refuge. Situated in the Judean mountains about eighty miles south of Nazareth, Hebron shares the rocky region with both Bethlehem and Jerusalem. This is why Scripture often speaks of travelers going "up" to Jerusalem. To reach the holy city, they would have to climb up the mountains on which it sat.

These Judean mountains are also the setting for many of the psalms of David, the hills to which he lifted his eyes in Psalm 121. In fact, this psalm is part of a larger collection known as the Psalms of Ascent (Ps. 120–134) that temple pilgrims sang as they climbed the mountains on their way to worship. Marked by dramatic cliffs and valleys, rocky outcroppings, and rough, crooked roads, the landscape becomes even more intriguing as the Christmas story unfolds.

When Mary finally arrives at Elizabeth's house, she calls out a greeting; in response, the child growing inside Elizabeth leaps with joy. This child is, of course, John, the one Gabriel promised would be "filled with the Holy Spirit while still in his mother's womb."[3] The one whose ministry would be to prepare the way of the Promised Son as described in Isaiah 40 and echoed in Luke 3:

> A voice of one crying out:
> Prepare the way of the LORD in the
>   wilderness;
> make a straight highway for our God in the
>   desert.
> Every valley will be lifted up,
> and every mountain and hill will be leveled;
> the uneven ground will become smooth
> and the rough places, a plain.
> And the glory of the LORD will appear,
> and all humanity together will see it.[4]

The call to "prepare the way of the Lord" was similar to the command a king might give at the start of a military campaign when he'd send crews and engineers to create a road before him. Keep in mind that leveling of mountains and filling of valleys is no small thing; it's the kind of work only a king could command. In much of Appalachia, for example, infrastructure projects like roads, dams, and bridges have historically taken the resources of the national government.

It's no coincidence, then, that the one whose ministry would be marked by the metaphorical filling up of valleys and leveling of mountains would know the mountains and valleys by heart. And it's no coincidence that Mary would respond to the yet-to-be-born John with her own song about how God levels things out. "My soul doth magnify the Lord," she sings, "And my spirit hath rejoiced in God my Saviour.

> For he hath regarded the low estate of his handmaiden. . . . He hath shewed strength with his arm; he hath scattered the proud in the imagination of their hearts. He hath put down the mighty from their seats, and exalted them of low degree.[5]

Mary knows that in the world's eyes she is nobody. She sits low in the hollow. But she also knows who her God is. She knows that he topples those who sit high and proud. She knows that he "lifts up the humble."[6] She knows that when the promised Son comes, every mountain will be leveled and every valley filled. All that is crooked and corrupt will be made straight, and the rough places, smooth. She knows that when the glory of the Lord appears, *everyone* will be able to see it together—regardless of where they sit on the landscape.

Because three months later, when John is finally born and his people gather round to celebrate, Zechariah finds his words again. And filled with the Holy Spirit, he proclaims:

> And you, child, will be called
> a prophet of the Most High,
> for you will go before the Lord
> to prepare his ways,
> to give his people knowledge of salvation
> through the forgiveness of their sins.
> Because of our God's merciful compassion,
> the dawn from on high will visit us
> to shine on those who live in darkness
> and the shadow of death,
> to guide our feet into the way of peace.[7]

This was their hope: The dawn was coming, even for those who sat behind the mountains in the shadows. All the obstacles, all the crookedness, all the sin that had hemmed them in and kept them from experiencing its light, would be removed. The world was about to be remade in the same cataclysmic way it was once created.

Today we cling to this same hope. So that even now as we wait in the shadows for Christ to reign in his fullness, we can sing in harmony with Isaiah, Mary, John, Zechariah, and all those who wait on their King: "Arise, shine for thy light is come, and the glory of the LORD is about to be revealed!"[8]

# 8

# Family Land

I grew up in Pennsylvania on ten acres of family land that had once been part of a larger plot of a couple hundred acres. But by the time I came along, the original farm had been sectioned off—either sold or parceled out through inheritance. My aunt and uncles each had their own acreage, but somehow we knew that the land belonged together. So, while our separate claims were always respected, I had free reign over the whole of it.

Here, in Virginia's Blue Ridge, the idea of "family land" or a "home place" is still understood, although fewer and fewer plots remain intact. Like my family's experience, once-large tracts have been whittled down through the generations or sold off when the last descendant moved out of the area. But even for those who want to stay, it's increasingly difficult. With the rise of industrial agriculture, smaller holdings struggle to make the land pay, and heaven help you if you're the great-great-great-grandchild tasked with keeping it together on your own.

So, when I read in Luke 2:4 that Joseph and Mary traveled to his hometown of Bethlehem "because he was of the house and family line of David," I know there's a story here.

Despite the initial background information about a census, scholars don't know exactly why Joseph had to travel *from* *Nazareth* to "his own town." If Bethlehem was Joseph's hometown, why wasn't he there already? Some suggest that Joseph actually lived in Bethlehem and had simply gone to Nazareth to bring Mary back home. But others think Joseph lived in

Nazareth, and, like so many of us, he was displaced from his family roots.

During the exilic period, the tribes of Israel had been scattered or taken captive to Assyria and Babylon. And while some were able to return, many found their land was handed off from one empire to another—much the same way indigenous peoples of North America found themselves removed from their ancestral homelands. It's also possible that Joseph's ancestors migrated to Nazareth for better long-term prospects, the way the Great Migration carried six million black Americans out of the South during the twentieth century. Or perhaps, like folks tend to do where I live, Joseph's people simply moved for work.

But roots run deep, and ties to the land remain. So regardless of the reason, when it came time to be counted, Joseph went to Bethlehem.

Theologically speaking, the reference to Bethlehem is an important link to David and presents Jesus as the Promised Son who would reign as King. As Gabriel told Mary, the child in her womb "will be great and will be called the Son of the Most High, and the Lord God will give him the throne of his father David.[1]

But there's something more. Luke makes a particular point to tell us that Jesus was only "thought to be the son of Joseph."[2] And having just established the virgin birth, he is not arguing from Joseph's biological parentage. But he might be hinting at something in Joseph's ancestry—a memory of a family story, one handed down through the generations—a story that helps us understand the unique role Joseph will play in the Promised Son's life. It is a story of family land and hard times. A story of when Bethlehem, "the house of bread," stood empty.

Located roughly six miles south of Jerusalem, Bethlehem sits on a large aquifer. This water source makes Bethlehem particularly fruitful, which explains its historic association with food, provision, and fertility—one that predates the Israelites' presence in Canaan. But during the time of the judges, a famine covered the land, and like so many others throughout history, Joseph's ancestors, Elimelech and Naomi, were forced away from their home in search of food. By the time the famine had lifted, Elimelech and his sons had died in Moab, leaving Naomi and her daughter-in-law, Ruth, alone and without heirs. Destitute, the two returned to Bethlehem at the beginning of harvest, facing the end of the family line and, according to the laws of inheritance, all claims to the family land.

Except for one thing. In the law, God provided for something known as a "levirate marriage." In such a marriage, a close relative of the deceased could marry a widow and raise their first son as the heir to her first husband. While both parties had to consent to the marriage, it was an act of particular sacrifice on the part of the "kinsman redeemer" to relinquish his claim to his son in order to save another's.

If you know the story of Ruth, you know how Ruth found herself gleaning in the field of a man named Boaz, how he turned out to be a close relative, and how Naomi counseled her to seek his favor. You also know how he willingly and eagerly offered himself as her redeemer. But you may also remember that another, closer relative also had claim on the land, one he was all too eager to actualize. Eager, that is, until he realized that to get the land, he'd have to marry Ruth and jeopardize his own inheritance in the process.

A friend of mine once remarked that how we care for the land often mirrors how we care for those dependent on it, especially women and children. Is our attitude one of entitlement and privilege? Do we see the land as serving us and our interests? Or is it one of stewardship and responsibility? Do we see the potential for life and goodness bound up in both?

In God's economy, inheritance is not about possession; it is about stewardship. Whatever we receive, we receive in trust, borrowing it from future generations. And so rather than preserving the ego of one man or expanding his wealth, the goal of the levirate marriage was to preserve a family and the land on which they depended. Even if it meant doing so at great personal cost.

Boaz did eventually marry Ruth, redeeming her and the family plot; and their first child—the one who would continue the line—was none other than Obed, the father of Jesse, the father of David, the great-great-great-great-grandfather of Joseph.

So when the angel appeared to Joseph over a millennium later and told him to take an already-pregnant Mary as his wife, God was inviting him to follow in the steps of his ancestor Boaz, to risk his good name and his own interests on behalf of another. God was inviting him to raise up a son who would redeem the family and the family land, saving his household from certain destruction. God was inviting him to mirror his own fatherly care.

If all this talk of male heirs and fatherhood feels not only archaic but like a way to preserve the legacy of patriarchal norms that have marginalized women for centuries, I understand. But if conception teaches us the shape of hope and faith, can I suggest that fatherhood teaches us the shape of *faithfulness*?

After all, when a woman conceives and gives birth, there is little question about who the mother is. But biology being what it is, a father must declare himself. A man must publicly take responsibility for a child and, in so doing, commit to love and provide for this new life. When Boaz answers the call to be Ruth's kinsman redeemer, when Joseph answers the call to stand by Mary and raise Jesus, when any other good man does the same, he is mirroring the faithfulness of God himself.

We do not call God "our Father" because he is man or because he has a male body. We call him Father because that is the closest language we have to describe what he has done by publicly taking responsibility for us, loving us, protecting us, and granting us a share in the divine inheritance. Unlike those who leave when they realize what it will cost them, our Father gives and gives and gives.

"What, then, are we to say about these things?" Paul asks in Romans 8.

> If God is for us, who is against us? He did not even spare his own Son but gave him up for us all. How will he not also with him grant us everything? . . . Who can separate us from the love of Christ? Can affliction or distress or persecution or famine or nakedness or danger or sword? . . . I am persuaded that neither death nor life, nor angels nor rulers, nor things present nor things to come, nor powers, nor height nor depth, nor any other created thing will be able to separate us from the love of God that is in Christ Jesus our Lord.[3]

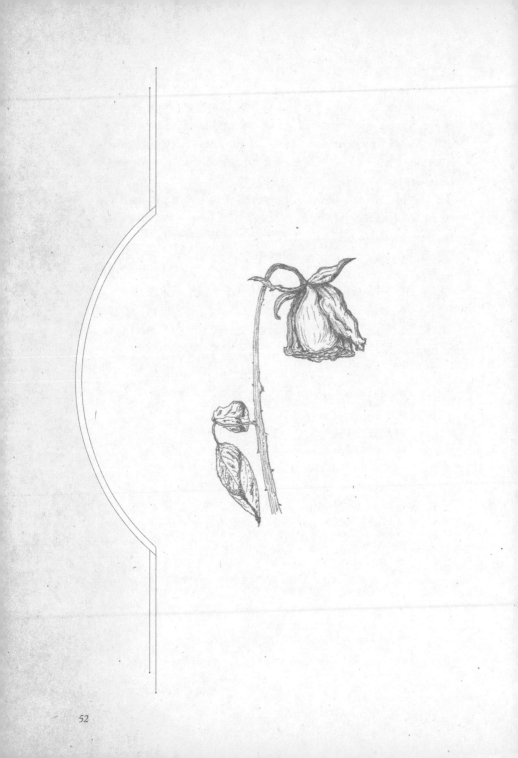

# 9

# Birth Pains

An old family cemetery sits about three hundred yards from our house. It's a quiet place, shaded by oaks and pines, and in spring the graves are covered in periwinkle. Some days I walk there, visiting with my neighbors even if we are separated by the centuries.

If you pay attention, you can make out the family constellations, who married whom and when, links between households intuited by maiden names that become middle names in the next generation. And if you learn to read between the lines, you can sometimes discern when tragedy struck—when too many death dates are too close together to be explained by natural causes. Or when two graves lie next to each other, the small one marked by a stone lamb or angel and the other with the words "beloved wife." Here you know that a newborn, perhaps only days or hours old, left the world as soon as they entered it, and their mother, weary of both body and soul, left with them.

Even after years of seeing such things, I'm always shocked—shocked by both their existence and their normalcy. Birth may be natural, as they say, but it has never been safe. So when the Scripture tells us that the time came for Mary to give birth, this is no small thing, especially in light of what the Promised Son was coming to do.

Because just moments after God promises that Eve's offspring will crush the head of the serpent, he tells her that her pain will "greatly multiply" and "in sorrow thou shalt bring forth children."[1] While newer Bible translations render *sorrow* as "pain" or "labor pains," this doesn't do justice to what a woman faces in pregnancy and birth. Just as God tells the man that his attempts to cultivate the earth would result in thorns and thistles, the woman's attempts to cultivate life through her body will be marked by disappointment, pain, loss, and even death itself.

So while Mary had the promise of a Son, there was no accompanying promise of her own safety. In fact, in the apocalyptic rendering of Jesus's birth found in Revelation 12, the apostle John sees a "great fiery red dragon"[2] standing in front of a woman in labor. Representing the devil, this red dragon will do anything to stop the Promised Son from coming into the world and is a threatening presence hovering over them in the very moments of delivery. Even after the child is born safely, the dragon continues to harass the woman, furious at her role in his birth.

When Mary answered the call of God with "I am the Lord's servant. May it be done to me according to your word,"[3] she agreed to a process that, in an earthly sense, had no guaranteed outcome. Beyond discomfort and pain, she also faced complications like preeclampsia, breech presentation, loss of blood, hemorrhaging of the uterine wall, and the ever-present threat of infection that could snatch her away even weeks after delivery.

Today in the developing world, such things rarely lead to death, but for most of history, death was a constant companion to birth without regard to class, education, or social status. Jane Seymour and Catherine Parr (two of Henry VIII's six wives) died as a result of childbirth as did Mary Wollstonecraft, who passed after giving birth to Mary Shelley, the author of *Frankenstein*. Martha Jefferson, Thomas Jefferson's wife, also succumbed from complications of childbirth, and poet Phillis Wheatley, the first woman and African American to be published in the New World, lies with her infant in an unmarked grave after she died the same way.

Not that Mary was unaware of the risks. She had undoubtedly known women lost in childbirth or at least heard the stories. And when she and Joseph traveled to Bethlehem, they likely passed in the vicinity of Rachel's tomb, which by that time had become something of a sacred site. The beloved wife of the patriarch Jacob, Rachel waited and longed for children only to die while giving birth to her second son, Benjamin. As Genesis 35 records,

> When they were still some distance from Ephrath, Rachel began to give birth, and her labor was difficult. . . . So Rachel died and was buried on the way to Ephrath (that is, Bethlehem). Jacob set up a marker on her grave; it is the marker at Rachel's grave still today."[4]

So when Mary's hour comes, it comes with both expectation and uncertainty. And with the earth itself, she groans, longing to be delivered.

But Mary's pain is not necessarily the point here—no more than any other suffering is an end in itself. Because in the wisdom of God, the child she gives birth to will reverse the very thing that threatens her. In the wisdom of God, childbirth itself will become one of the ways we understand the Promised Son's work in the world and within us. In the wisdom of God, we will be reborn through faith in him.

Make no mistake. The pain is real. The danger is real. But so is faith in God's promises, and so is the joy that follows.

Because as soon as Luke tells us that Mary's time has come, he also tells us that she gave birth.

She gave birth.

She gave birth.

She gave birth.

After all the years, after all the waiting, after all the longing and disappointed dreams, after all the loss, all the pain, and all the struggle, the Promised Son is finally here. He has come. And faith is made sight.

There's a curious passage in 1 Timothy. Speaking in context of the character of men and women of faith, Paul alludes to the fall, writing that "the woman [Eve] was deceived and transgressed. But she will be saved through childbearing, if they continue in faith, love, and holiness, with good sense."[5]

Given Paul's teachings about salvation across the New Testament, it's unlikely that Paul is teaching a form of maternal regeneration here; namely, that the act of giving birth somehow spiritually saves a woman. So some scholars suggest that he's combating the surrounding pagan culture that promised fertility goddesses would keep women safe in childbirth. Instead of offering worship to Artemis (or Diana, as she was known to the Romans), Christian women were to look to God in faith, just as Eve and Mary had done before them.

But another reading is possible. That both men and women alike would be saved through *the* childbirth—the birth of the Promised Son. A birth that will eventually break the curse that holds sway over birthing itself. In this sense, the curse of Genesis 3 is not God's final word. And to prove this, "when the time came to completion, God sent his Son, born of a woman."[6]

Perhaps it seems odd that childbirth, and not war or public policy, initiates redemption. Perhaps it seems odd that God would use the woman who was deceived to bring the One who would crush the deceiver. But this is the mystery of God's work, and even more unexpected is the fact that Jesus likens his own death to what a woman experiences when she gives birth. "You will become sorrowful," Jesus tells his disciples just hours before he is crucified, "but your sorrow will turn to joy. When a woman is in labor, she has pain because her time has come. But when she has given birth to a child, she no longer remembers the suffering because of the joy that a person has been born into the world."[7]

So for the joy set before *him*, Jesus comes into the world, lives among us, and endures the suffering of the cross—all to bring us to life.

And having been born through the suffering of another, we enter into suffering the same way he did, entrusting ourselves to the Father and believing that we

> are being guarded by God's power through faith for a salvation that is ready to be revealed in the last time. You rejoice in this, even though now for a short time, if necessary, you suffer grief in various trials so that the proven character of your faith . . . may result in praise, glory, and honor at the revelation of Jesus Christ.[8]

# 10

# Evergreen

Sometime after Thanksgiving and before the first weekend in December, we'll climb the steps into a freezing attic and carry down the storage boxes that hold our holiday decorations. Inside are strings of lights, a constantly evolving nativity set, stockings to hang on the mantle, and of course, years of carefully packed ornaments for the Christmas tree. Soon we'll pile into the car and head further up into the mountains to where the hillsides grow in neat rows of blue spruce, Fraser fir, and white pine. We'll debate the merits of each, find one that is sufficiently tall and shapely, and cut it fresh from the ground.

While evergreens are synonymous with Christmas celebrations today, it wasn't always this way. Brought to the American colonies by German immigrants, Christmas trees really didn't become widespread until the late 1800s, in part because a more famous German immigrant, Prince Albert, popularized them in England when he married Queen Victoria. Prior to this, Christmas trees were regarded, at best, as a distinctly German tradition and, at worst, a pagan one.

Throughout church history, there's always been a tension about how and how much of surrounding culture to incorporate into religious celebration. Because ancient cultures often worshipped the earth itself, putting faith in trees, wind, sun, and water, their celebrations included natural imagery and greenery. But such celebrations were also marked by violence, drunkenness, and licentious behavior. So when your surrounding culture is pantheistic and violent, what role should nature play in worship?

Ironically, the tension between worshipping creation and worshipping *with* creation is at the heart of the legend of the first Christmas tree.

While many credit Martin Luther with introducing Christmas trees, the tradition goes back much further to the early 700s and an English missionary named Winfried who preached the gospel in what is now Germany. Also known by his Latin name, Saint Boniface, historical records confirm that Winfried's ministry laid the groundwork for the church in Northern Europe. But in an 1897 retelling of the legend of the first Christmas tree, author and Presbyterian minister Henry van Dyke renders Winfried as a woodsman missionary, a kind of medieval, monastic Paul Bunyan, who traverses the Germanic wilds, shod in leather boots, wrapped in furs, and shouldering a thick, wooden staff.

One wintry Christmas Eve, the story goes, Winfried enters a village where he sees its inhabitants gathered around a magnificent tree known as Odin's Oak. Generations have worshipped under its branches, feeding it the blood of sacrifices to gain their god's favor. But tonight, there will be a special sacrifice, a costly one, precious enough to prove their devotion. The sacrifice of the young, firstborn son of the village chieftain.

Just as the village priest raises his stone hammer to crush the child's skull, Winfried rushes forward and thrusts his staff against the weapon, sending it flying. "Not a life shall be blotted out in the darkness to-night," van Dyke writes, "but the great shadow of the tree which hides you from the light of heaven shall be swept away. For this is the birth-night of the . . . Christ, son of the All-Father, and Saviour of mankind. Fairer is He than Baldur the Beautiful, greater than Odin the Wise, kinder than Freya the Good. Since He has come to earth the bloody sacrifice must cease."[1]

Winfried then lays his ax to the trunk of Odin's oak. As he does, a mighty wind from heaven picks up the oak and with a giant crack, fells it. Winfried tells the villagers to use the wood to build a church and then calls their attention to a small evergreen, "standing straight and green, with its top pointing toward the stars, amid the divided ruins of the fallen oak.

> Here is the living tree, with no stain of blood upon it, that shall be the sign of your new worship. See how it points to the sky. Call it the tree of the Christ-child. Take it up and carry it to the chieftain's hall. You shall go no more into the shadows of the forest to keep your feasts with secret rites of shame. You shall keep them at home, with laughter and songs and rites of love."[2]

Or that's how the story goes, at least.

Despite the historical details of van Dyke's narrative, it's not hard to see the biblical themes: a tree that becomes a place of worship, the evergreen that points to God and eternity, and the impending sacrifice of a firstborn son.

In fact, the motif of the sacrificial son is woven throughout Scripture from the earliest pages. In Genesis 3, the Promised Son will crush the serpent's head, but he will be bruised in the process. God calls Abraham to offer up Isaac. The firstborn sons of Israel are spared in the Exodus, but the firstborn sons of the Egyptians are taken. The law taught that God had a claim on the life of the firstborn male, and that the son must be redeemed or bought back from the Lord by way of a tax and circumcision.[3] And Hannah returns her miraculous firstborn son, Samuel, to the Lord's service.

By the time we reach Luke 2 and read that Mary "brought forth her firstborn son,"[4] it's not simply a statement about gendered birth order. There's something more going on here, something on which all our Christian celebrations depend and why it's fitting that we celebrate this season with evergreens as a sign of eternal life. Because Mary's firstborn son is also the *eternal* Son of God.

In human terms, to be a son implies time. A son is always younger than his father, the next installment in a chronological line. But when we speak of the second person of the Trinity, of God the Son, we're not speaking in terms of time or even status. We're not saying that the Son is somehow younger than the Father or even beneath him. While we are beings locked in time, God exists outside of time, and his eternality encompasses both eternity future and eternity past. In orthodox Trinitarianism, God the Father, God the Son, and God the Holy Spirit exist simultaneously, outside of time in perfect union and communion. As the writer of Hebrews says, "Jesus Christ is the same yesterday, today, and forever."[5]

So why do we call Jesus "God the Son"?

In part, the language of Father, Son, and Holy Spirit allows us to differentiate between the three persons of the Trinity. But the language of Father and Son also allows us to *affirm* that the Son, though different from the Father, is the same as the Father. Similarly to how a human man has a human son, a divine Father has a divine Son, with all the characteristics and authority that makes him divine in the first place. Or as the Nicene Creed put it, hundreds of years before Winfried's confrontation in a German wood:

> We believe in one Lord, Jesus Christ,
> the only Son of God,
> eternally begotten of the Father,
> God from God, Light from Light,
> true God from true God,

begotten, not made,
of one Being with the Father.
Through him all things were made.
For us and for our salvation
he came down from heaven:
by the power of the Holy Spirit he became
    incarnate from the Virgin Mary,
and was made man.[6]

The miracle of the incarnation is that the timeless Son entered time. God the eternal Son became Mary's firstborn son. The Creator became part of the creation and submits himself as a man to God the Father and, in doing so, also becomes "the firstborn among many brethren."[7]

Then, as a good and faithful firstborn Son, he takes responsibility to care for and protect his Father's household. He takes responsibility for the future of family and the earth that is their home. Instead of a human sacrifice to appease the creation at the foot of an oak tree, God the Son sacrifices himself on a tree on behalf of his creation. And because he died, we, his earthly brothers and sisters, have an inheritance of evergreen, eternal life.

These are deep questions and deeper realities—ones we ultimately accept by faith. But our weak and doubting faith is no match for the faithfulness of the Eternal One who became Mary's firstborn Son. And so we trust him, and not in our own understanding. We trust Jesus who is "the radiance of God's glory and the exact expression of his nature, sustaining all things by his powerful word."[8] We trust that the One who existed from eternity will keep us forevermore.

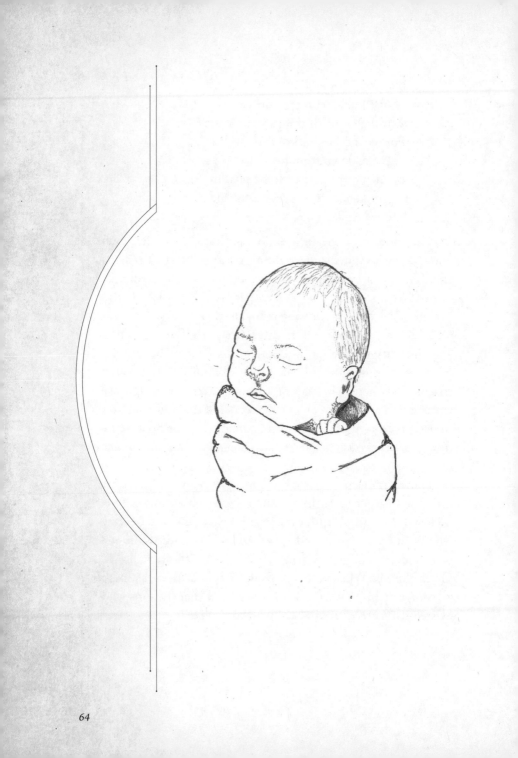

# 11

# Swaddling Bands

H ow did you sleep?"
      Nathan greets me with these words almost every morning. It's a dangerous question because while I often sleep well enough, some mornings he'll get the director's cut of the previous eight hours. How I couldn't fall asleep and then I woke up because I had to use the bathroom. How my dreams were layered and unsettling. How the cat startled me at four o'clock and how I lay there for another hour writing an email or essay in my head. How I eventually fell asleep only to hear the alarm go off an hour later.

To be fair, I've never been a particularly good sleeper— never been much good at stillness. But years of motherhood, of getting up with babies in all hours of night, did me in. My ears are inexorably tuned to the faintest sound of distress. My mind is constantly trying to remember who needs what and when, and I find it nearly impossible to nod off without a book in hand. So I'm not exaggerating when I tell you that one of the best Christmas gifts I've ever received was a quality fifteen-pound weighted blanket.

Originally created for occupational therapy, weighted blankets are filled with plastic or glass pellets, and when they are draped over a hyperstimulated body, they can help it relax or, in my case, fall and stay asleep. While more research is needed, these blankets work on theory that something called "deep touch pressure" helps the body regulate itself when under physical and emotional distress. Deep touch pressure includes physical sensations like a firm handshake or hug, stroking, petting animals, or even wrapping a sore muscle in an elastic bandage. While very light touch like tickling stimulates the nervous system, deep pressure touch actually relaxes and calms it.

You can achieve this kind of deep pressure by a weighted blanket, a twenty-second hug (proven to stimulate oxytocin production), or special compression clothing that squeezes and holds a body tightly. Deep pressure is also the phenomenon behind infant swaddling and might help explain why Mary wrapped the newborn Jesus "tightly in cloth."[1]

These "swaddling clothes" or "swaddling bands," as some Bible versions translate the Greek word *esparganōsen*, were long strips of cloth, similar to bandages. And in first-century Palestine, they were the standard in infant care. Soon after birth, the umbilical cord would have been cut, the infant washed clean of blood and vernix, rubbed with salt (believed to purify and prepare the baby's skin for the elements), and wrapped tightly in cloth strips in much the same way you might picture a mummy being wrapped. So common was this confining practice that the second-century Greek physician Galen cited it in his writings;[2] Ezekiel 16:4 mentions it as a sign of care and provision; and Job 38:9 uses it as a metaphor to explain how God restricts the waters of the earth to certain places.

As interesting as this is, it becomes even more so when you realize that Luke's record of Mary wrapping her son "tightly in cloth" is the first record we have of the incarnated body of the Son of God. The first thing you learn about Jesus's physical humanity is his need for comfort and care.

Because while these "swaddling clothes" served the obvious purpose of covering an infant's nakedness, they also help a newborn transition from the womb to the world. For the nine months prior to birth, a child knows only the stable, warm environment of his mother's body. He sleeps in a tight ball with every need effortlessly supplied. He does not know hunger because nourishment flows continuously through the umbilical cord. His senses are developed, meaning he is able to detect all sorts of sensory input, but this input is muted for now. It is quiet, dark, compact, and peaceful.

Then suddenly, birth ushers him into a world of intense, immediate physical sensation. His tender skin is exposed. His senses bombarded—every touch, taste, smell, sound, and sight is amplified a hundred times over. Lacking muscle coordination and the physical boundaries that once hemmed him in, he thrashes in the limitless open space of his new environment. He has no control over his sphincter or bladder.

Now imagine this. The God of the universe condescends to take on human flesh, choosing to come to earth as a baby. But to do this, he must cede control, even control over his own body. So that when he finally enters the world, he is at its complete mercy. Naked and disoriented, his arms and legs flail. His chest rises and falls. His heart races. He gasps for air. He screams out in confusion. His bladder empties, and his bowels flush meconium.

So his mother does what any good mother would do: she cares for him. She washes him. She covers his nakedness. She wraps him tightly, knowing this will calm him both body and soul. She draws him close. And suddenly his muscles begin to relax, his heart beats slower, his circulation improves. His brain releases dopamine and serotonin. His breathing is softer now. He shudders and hiccups and, with one final whimper, falls asleep, safe in his mother's arms.

When I think of how Mary clothed the body of this infant Jesus, it reminds me of how God clothed the naked bodies of Adam and Eve. After they'd eaten the forbidden fruit,

Genesis 3:7 says that instantly "the eyes of both of them were opened, and they knew they were naked." Just as birth moves a baby from one reality to another, their sin unexpectedly ushered them into a new existence. And in the blazing light of righteousness, they stand vulnerable, exposed, and ashamed. Flailing, they try to hide themselves, but everything is out of their control. Every nerve on edge, every sensation heightened, anxiety and trauma course through their bodies. They are disoriented and helpless, the curse of the world already pressing in on them from without, and the curse of sin warring from within.

But then Genesis says this: "The LORD God made clothing from skins for the man and his wife, and he clothed them."[3]

*And he clothed them.*

You might be tempted to read this as God being embarrassed or ashamed of their bodies—that their nakedness offended him somehow. Or you might read a kind of irritation into it, as if God begrudgingly stepped in to solve a problem he had not created. But reading it this way would miss the heart of a good Father.

"Can a woman forget her nursing child," God asks in Isaiah 49, "or lack compassion for the child of her womb? Even if these forget, yet I will not forget you."[4] And then later in Isaiah 66, he promises: "As a mother comforts her son, so I will comfort you, and you will be comforted in Jerusalem."[5]

And so he clothed them. He covered them. He comforted them.

Just as Mary received, welcomed, and cared for her son, God receives, welcomes, and cares for us, his sons and daughters. Seeing us helpless and exposed, he clothes us, wrapping us tightly in the bands of his merciful compassion. Even when we have only ourselves to blame.

So certain is the Father's care for us that Jesus himself asks why we worry about it. "Observe how the wildflowers of the field grow. . . . If that's how God clothes the grass of the field, which is here today and thrown into the furnace tomorrow, won't he do much more for you—you of little faith?"[6]

So certain is the Father's care for us, all we need do is look at the cross. Because there, the Promised Son is once again stripped and exposed for us.

So certain is the Father's care for us, all we need do is look at the tomb to see the grave clothes folded, the Son's work of redemption complete.[7]

So certain is the Father's care for us that one day, when he gathers us together in a "vast multitude from every nation, tribe, people, and language," we will stand before him clothed in white—clothed in his righteousness, mercy, and compassion.[8]

And so today with eyes of faith, we learn to trust this care. We learn to trust that the God who clothed and comforted his restless children in the garden—the God who was clothed as a restless child—will do the same for us. We trust that the bands of his everlasting love will hold us secure, today and for eternity.

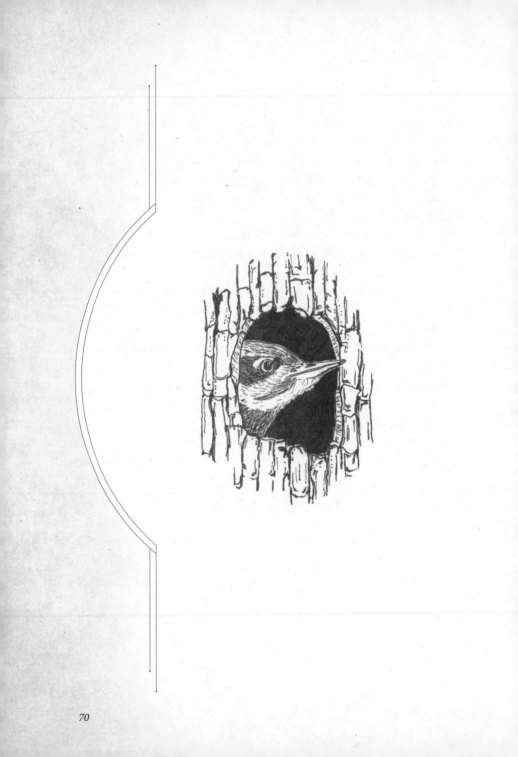

# 12

# No Room

**I**f you get to know Nathan, one of the first things you'll learn about him is that he is a birder. It wasn't always the case. When we first met, he had affection for nature, including birds, but in the last ten years, that affection has turned to a passion for our winged neighbors. On Monday nights you can find him swapping sightings at the local ornithological society. He has an app that informs him when rare birds are spotted in the area, and it's not unusual for an alert to send him racing out the door with camera and binoculars in hand. As our kids long ago learned, family vacation will most definitely include visits to nature preserves and wildlife sanctuaries.

So when news came last year that the U.S. Fish and Wildlife Service was planning to move the ivory-billed woodpecker from the "critically endangered" list to the "extinct" list, it was met—in our house at least—with the proper solemnity it deserved. Besides the obvious, designating a species extinct also means that funds will no longer be allocated for its preservation or its habitat protected. Any ivory-billed woodpeckers that might be hiding deep in the southern swamps and woodlands are now on their own.

To be fair, the fate of the ivory-billed woodpecker has been uncertain for over a hundred years. It was first registered as endangered in the late 1800s, and the last confirmed sighting occurred in 1944. Since then, there have been possible sightings with some being more likely than others. But even those that didn't turn out to be pileated woodpeckers (a smaller, more common look-alike) couldn't be sufficiently verified to meet the standards of the ornithological world.

Native to the southeastern United States, the ivory-billed woodpecker's range once stretched from the coastal plans of the Carolinas to the wetlands of East Texas. And while it was hunted, its extinction is primarily due to loss of habitat. Woodpeckers need wood after all. And for the ivory-billed woodpecker, home was found in old-growth forests filled with dead and decaying cypress trees whose trunks offered up a plentiful supply of larvae while their cavities proved just right for nesting.

Within the natural world, loss of suitable habitat can be a sign of impending doom because animals need the things a healthy environment provides: food, shelter, mating grounds, and the ability to safely raise young. Lose the things that support life, and it's only a matter of time before you lose life itself. This is why conservation efforts go beyond trying to save individual birds to preserving territory and range. It's not enough to catch the remaining members of a species and hold them in an artificial environment like a zoo or wildlife park. Living things were created to live off of and in harmony with their unique environment.

The importance of habitat to a species's survival may surprise you, especially after you've heard so much about nature's adaptability, but we humans actually face a similar threat. In the famed hierarchy of needs, shelter ranks beside food and clothing as a first-tier biological necessity. And as anyone who has grown up without a stable home or basic housing can tell you, the effects of their absence are far-reaching.

When you understand the significance of a safe environment, you'll begin to understand Luke's point in telling us that Mary laid her newborn child in a manger "because there was no guest room available for them."[1] Having come to Bethlehem to participate in the census, Joseph and Mary find the town full of others doing the same. So with suitable habitat scarce, they eventually find refuge in a space that also sheltered animals (as per the mention of a manger).

Scholars debate whether that space was a stable, the ground floor of a relative's home, or a cave. Church tradition has historically interpreted Jesus's birthplace as a cave or grotto, and if you visit Bethlehem today, you'll find a church built over the supposed place of his birth. But regardless of where he was born, the *meaning* of Luke's words are clear. Having just left the hospitable environment of Mary's womb, Jesus enters a world struggling to support life. A world that has "no room" for him.

It's easy to miss the significance of this, especially if you're reading those words in a warm house filled with abundance in eager anticipation of the holidays. With our physical needs met, it would be tempting to interpret "no room" as an emotional or relational alienation. A kind of social snub or lack of hospitality, the world rejecting her rightful King. And in one sense, this is true. The apostle John writes in his Gospel that "he was in the world, and the world was created through him, and yet the world did not recognize him. He came to his own, and his own people did not receive him."[2]

But I wonder if the significance of there being "no room" to house Joseph, Mary, and the baby Jesus is more basic—so basic, in fact, that those of us who are insulated from scarcity miss it. To say there was "no room" is a statement about the limits of the environment and the limits of resources. It is a statement about the world Jesus came to redeem, a world where an entire species might die for lack of a home.

In this sense, the words *no room* echo through the totality of the fallen creation as a kind of existential threat. It is a threat that began when Adam and Eve were first dispelled from their garden home, forced to wander east of Eden. A threat that Abraham shouldered when God called him to a place yet unknown. A threat that stalked the children of Israel as they traveled in the wilderness. A threat that became all too true when their descendants were scattered in exile. And it was a threat that Jesus himself faced throughout his life and ministry on this earth.

Because some thirty years later, when a certain confident scribe promised: "I will follow you wherever you go," Jesus stopped him with these words: "Foxes have dens, and birds of the sky have nests, but the Son of Man has no place to lay his head."[3]

*Friend, you don't understand what you're saying. You don't understand what it means to follow me. You don't understand that, from my earliest days, there has been "no room" for me. You don't understand what I've come to do and what it has cost me. You don't understand that I wander homeless so I can make a true and proper home for all who come to me in faith.*

So too, if we are to follow Jesus, we must learn to inhabit the world as he does. We must acknowledge that those of us who enjoy warm homes and safe environments are the minority. We must realize that the call of Christ sometimes means leaving houses and lands just as he did. And we must accept that loving a world where there is "no room" will not necessarily lead to domestic tranquility. Not directly, at least.

Because as we learn to let go of such things, as we learn to love him above all the earth can offer us, he will give us what we truly long for. "If anyone loves me, he will keep my word," Jesus says. "My Father will love him, and we will come to him and make our home with him."[4]

This promise frees us to follow him wherever he leads. We do not need to cling to houses and lands because our home is with him. And to those who follow in this narrow way, he makes another promise:

> Don't let your heart be troubled. Believe in God; believe also in me. In my Father's house are many rooms. If it were not so, would I have told you that I am going to prepare a place for you? If I go away and prepare a place for you, I will come again and take you to myself, so that where I am you may be also.[5]

And so by faith, we receive the promise. By faith, we believe in God, and we believe in Christ also, counting him faithful to care for us even when the world around us does not.

By faith we profess that those who have left all to follow him will gain a hundred times more. By faith we will wander as strangers and pilgrims who are seeking a better home. We will leave houses built on sand for those built on the One who was laid in a stone manager. We will trust the One who promises to make room for us. Until that day when we are all gathered together in his Father's house, safe and secure, forevermore.

# 13

# Among the Beasts

Our family is the proud keeper of an elegant, black-and-white cat named Francis. He came home with us after my son and I made an impromptu stop at the SPCA. We didn't go with the intention of bringing anyone home, but Francis was determined to come and made it clear with his beguiling purrs, head butts, and marking us as his own. It's one of the best decisions we've ever made.

Francis is not a perfect cat, but he is clean, quiet, and well-mannered. His only bad habit consists of bringing small wildlife inside during the spring and summer. But knowing that he's just trying to please us, we forgive him, and I find myself only mildly annoyed when chasing a sparrow around the living room or retrieving a baby bunny from behind the piano. There is one thing, however. . . .

It began shortly after we brought home a golden retriever puppy (also for my son). Ben is sweet-natured, friendly, and easily trained, but adding him to the household was like adding jet fuel to a fire. Extraordinarily clumsy and insatiably curious, he tears around corners, scarfs down food, clambers up and down the steps, and is generally too much.

One evening, with Ben safely tucked away in his crate, Francis came padding into my bedroom where I was reading. Patient and well-mannered as always, he sat at my feet and gave a quiet meow. After waiting an appropriate amount of time, he added another. I looked up from my book, and we made eye contact. He mewed once more and then turned to leave, almost as if inviting me to follow. So I did. (When a cat asks you to follow him, you really don't have a choice.)

He continued silently down the hall and led me to the kitchen and his feeding dish. He sat down, looked up at me, and again meowed. Not being entirely sure what was happening, I checked his water, which was clean and fresh, and made sure that his bowl was full. When he turned to eat, I turned to leave and went back to my bedroom and my book.

But no sooner had I found my place than Francis was once again at my feet. He politely meowed, and when I didn't look up quickly enough, he tapped my leg with one of his mittened paws. Satisfied that he finally had my attention, he turned and walked down the hall toward the kitchen. Again I followed. (When a cat asks you to follow him for a *second* time, you do it, and if given the opportunity, apologize for having failed to understand his request the first time.)

He led me again to his food dish, stopping occasionally to turn his head to make sure I was present. And before settling into eat, he gave me one last look to confirm I understood. Obviously I didn't and returned to my bedroom and my book. So for a third time, Francis came to find me, and for a third time, he sat calmly at my feet and mewed. But this time I swear I heard him sigh.

"What do you want?" I responded in exasperation. "I don't know what you want!"

To which my daughter, upon hearing me talk to the cat, opened her bedroom door and yelled, "He wants you to keep watch over him while he eats. He's scared."

While we don't know where Joseph and Mary ultimately found refuge, the Scripture makes a point to tell us that Mary laid her firstborn Son in a manger, a stone trough or slab used to feed animals. From our modern standpoint, this underscores the destitute circumstances into which Jesus was born, and while this is likely true, the manger signals something else as well.

The manger is where a master cares for his animals. In fact, feeding and sheltering domesticated animals is one of the most basic responsibilities of animal husbandry, forming an almost unbreakable bond between master and beast. Whenever Francis goes on an extended outdoor wander and the children worry, I simply shrug and say, "He knows where he's fed."

In the best cases, this human-animal bond is healthy and serves to strengthen the relationship. The prophet Isaiah even mentions the trust animals have for those who care for them, contrasting it to Israel's lack of trust in God. In Isaiah 1:3, he writes: "The ox knows its owner, and the donkey its master's feeding trough, but Israel does not know [me]; my people do not understand." So reading that Jesus is laid in a *manger* signals something about provision and trust—the kind of provision a good, righteous master offers those who depend on him.

To understand the full significance, though, you'll need to remember something about Adam. When God made the first man and woman in his own image, he gave them stewardship of the animals. Genesis 2 records a curious account of God bringing the animals to Adam to see what he would call them. "And whatever the man called a living creature, that was its name. The man gave names to all the livestock, to the birds of the sky, and to every wild animal."[1]

The naming of the animals establishes Adam as the steward of these beasts, but it also shows that the beasts recognize him as their master. So when the Promised Son comes to fulfill all the first Adam failed to do—and when that same Promised Son is placed in a manager—we need to pay attention. Here's how the apostle Paul explains Jesus's work as the new and better Adam:

> For if by the one man's trespass the many
> died, how much more have the grace of God
> and the gift which comes through the grace
> of the one man Jesus Christ overflowed to
> the many. . . . But where sin multiplied, grace
> multiplied even more.[2]

Of course, we experience the second Adam's overflowing grace in certain ways as human beings, but I wonder if we're too quick to limit the scope of his grace. I wonder if we forget that "He comes to make His blessings flow/Far as the curse is found"[3]—even when the curse affects the beasts he has made. Lest you think I'm being too fanciful here, consider the words of Psalm 104:

> How countless are your works, LORD!
> In wisdom you have made them all;
> the earth is full of your creatures. . . .
> All of them wait for you
> to give them their food at the right time.
> When you give it to them,
> they gather it;
> when you open your hand,
> they are satisfied with good things.[4]

Yes, the manger signals something about this baby, but it is not simply his poverty. By being placed in the manger, he is revealed as both the rightful son of Adam charged with caring for his creation and also the eternal Son of God who created them and who provides for them. So instead of filling the manger with hay or corn, he fills it with himself.

But there's something more. During his earthly ministry, Jesus uses God's care for the animals to prove his care for us. "Consider the birds of the sky," he challenges the people.

"They don't sow or reap or gather into barns, yet your heavenly Father feeds them. Aren't you worth more than they?"[5]

If God provides for even the *animals*, you can be confident he will provide for you. And the fact that Jesus was laid in an animal's feeding trough means that he's going to feed you, too. He is a good Master who takes care of those who depend on him. You are safe with him. You can rest easy. You may wander, but deep down you know where you are fed.

But we must receive this promise by faith and live believing it is true. Because Jesus continues:

> So don't worry, saying, "What will we eat?" or "What will we drink?" or "What will we wear?" For the Gentiles eagerly seek all these things, and your heavenly Father knows that you need them. But seek first the kingdom of God and his righteousness, and all these things will be provided for you.[6]

In this world, where chaos and scarcity reign, we must do as Francis does—we must trust that our good Master is watching over us. We must trust that the One who promises to give us our daily bread is the same One who eventually sacrificed his own body and blood, inviting us to feast on the cup and bread. And so with all the wild beasts and all the animals gathered around their master's crib, we wait on him. We trust his care, knowing that he will give us food at the right time and that he will satisfy our soul with all good things.

# 14

# Keeping Watch

There's a stillness to the late night hours. The house, bustling and bursting with activity just hours ago, now lies silent. My children sleep in their beds, and I can hear Nathan's breathing, deep and low—the sound of honest rest.

But I'm awake. I can't tell you exactly why because there are too many reasons. Perhaps I didn't get enough activity during the day, or I watched a movie too late. Maybe I'm just thinking about everything again. But I'm awake, wrapped in a blanket, sitting in the quiet of my living room.

After eighteen years of such midnight wakings, ones that began with my daughter's birth, I'm no longer surprised to find myself here in the darkness. Somehow she and her brothers learned how to sleep through the night even as I forgot. But if I'm honest, I don't mind. It's become a familiar place for me and ironically enough, a place of comfort.

When I was a young mother, I remember hearing my friends talk about how their husbands would wake up to get the baby or fix a bottle or just be present. But for the most part, that wasn't our story, and I never really cared that it wasn't. Nathan sleeps too heavily to hear a baby's cry, so by the time I'd wake him up to help, I was already awake myself. It never made sense for both of us to lose sleep, and since I had a more flexible schedule, I'd be the one to stumble to the nursery. I'd gather up my little one, and the two of us would curl up on a bed or couch. She'd nurse herself back to sleep while

I'd sit marveling at this fragile, helpless being who craved my presence in the darkest hours of the night.

I know other people have different stories and different needs. And if you're reading this through bleary, sleep-deprived eyes, I know the nights are long and hard. But years of being up in the middle of the night have also shaped me in unusual ways. When I find myself awake with my people safely sleeping, I'm inexplicably content and count myself blessed to keep watch over them.

This work of the midnight hours, of keeping watch over vulnerable things, becomes an important motif in the Christmas story. Panning out from the holy family, Luke now leads us through the darkened streets of Bethlehem, outside the city walls to the fields that surround David's hometown. There, among the rocky outcroppings and rugged hills, we find shepherds in the fields guarding their sheep through the night.

Some scholars think they are resting in fields that were recently harvested. After the farmer had stored his crop and the poor had gleaned their allotted portion, shepherds were invited to pasture their animals on last bits of grain and vegetation. The sheep and goats' hooves would churn and work the soil while their droppings fertilized it, preparing it for the next growing season. During these weeks, shepherds camped out in the fields overnight.

Others think that these fields are simply the pastures that surrounded Bethlehem, and like David so many years before, these shepherds were young boys tasked with leading their flock to new grazing land each day. They would live among the sheep, almost as one of them, roaming together and spending nights under the stars. And indeed, in 1 Samuel, whenever anyone is looking for young David, it seems like he's always out "tending the sheep."[1]

In either case, we find the shepherds awake in the night. While everyone else sleeps, they're keeping watch, protecting their flock from the dangers that lurk in the shadows. The threats are greatest after dark when predators like lions, bears, wolves, and jackals hunt and prowl. Moonless nights are especially dangerous because they give these nocturnal predators an advantage, their nighttime vision being so much sharper than the lambs' or even of those who protect them.

So these shepherds are on guard, vigilant and alert. Perhaps they take turns watching, grabbing a few hours of sleep here and there. And perhaps, like I did as a young mother, they make up for it during the day, dozing on the hills under the warmth of a high sun as their sheep safely graze.

But, I wonder, who keeps watch over them? Who protects the protectors? Who takes care of those who care for others? Who defends parents, pastors, teachers, guardians, and caregivers—all those whose vocations call them to be strong and alert to the threats lurking in darkness? Because if I've learned anything over the years, it's that my watchfulness is never enough. My ability to foresee or forestall danger always falls short. And my eyes become heavy, and my head nods, and more times than I care to remember, I fall asleep holding the very one I'm called to care for.

"I lift my eyes toward the mountains. Where will my help come from?" the shepherd-king asks in Psalm 121.[2] But then the answer comes sure and swift:

> My help comes from the LORD,
> the Maker of heaven and earth.
>
> He will not allow your foot to slip;
> your Protector will not slumber.
> Indeed, the Protector of Israel
> does not slumber or sleep.

The LORD protects you;
the LORD is a shelter right by your side.
The sun will not strike you by day
or the moon by night.

The LORD will protect you from all harm;
he will protect your life.
The LORD will protect your coming and
   going
both now and forever.[3]

Psalm 121 was the first psalm I taught my children when they were old enough to remember such things, and I can still hear their tiny voices reciting it. For some reason, in those early years, this was the psalm I most needed them to know, the truth I most needed to pass on: *In the night watches, as I watch over you, Someone greater is watching over both of us.*

I like to imagine that the shepherds in the Bethlehem fields knew this psalm by heart, too—that those who watched in the same fields as David did knew David's God was watching them. But even if they didn't, God knew them. And God saw their work.

There's a particular irony to vocations that call us to keep watch in the night. If everyone is asleep, who can see how hard you work? It's not that you're looking for praise; you just don't want to be overlooked. You don't want to go unnoticed and unseen. But it's all too easy to miss the work that happens in the darkness. It's all too easy to forget about those out in the fields with the flock.

But God does not forget. "God is not unjust," the author of Hebrews promises, "he will not forget your work and the love you demonstrated for his name."[4] Because in God's kingdom, those who serve in shadows are just as important as those who stand in the limelight. And nothing proves this more than the fact that God sends the news of the Promised Son to shepherds in the fields keeping watch over their flock by night. To them he sends the message of a Baby resting safely in a manger who is Christ the Lord. To them he entrusts "good news of great joy that will be for all the people."[5]

One day this same baby would grow up to become the Good Shepherd, who keeps watch through the night guarding those he loves. One day this baby would confront the evil that stalks in the shadows, laying down his life for his sheep to protect them. And one day he would be raised up again because the Father sees such sacrifices and honors them. "Therefore, my dear brothers and sisters, be steadfast, immovable, always excelling in the Lord's work, because you know that your labor in the Lord is not in vain."[6]

So knowing that the Father is watching over us, we will keep watch over those he has entrusted to us. Knowing that he never slumbers nor sleeps, we will let ourselves rest in his care. And knowing that he does not overlook our work, we will continue on, until the day when "the wolf and the lamb will feed together, and the lion will eat straw like cattle"[7] and all our watching will be ended.

And then, with the night passed and the dawn arising, we will find our joy complete.

# 15

# The Good Shepherd

A s I write this, a seventy-pound golden retriever sits at my feet. More accurately, he sits *on* my feet and is pressing the full weight of his body against my legs. And the only reason he's sitting on my feet is because he's grown too big to sit on my lap. Every morning Ben greets us as if we've been away for weeks. If my son does not wake up early enough for his liking, he sits outside his room and whines. When I close my office door to work, he lies beside it until I'm done. And in the evening when we sit down to watch television, he always finds a way to squeeze onto the couch, making room for himself where none exists.

In all fairness to Ben, dogs are naturally social creatures that live and hunt in packs. And if anything, we human beings are responsible for cultivating this instinct when we invited them into our lives as companions and workmates thousands of years ago. Ben himself comes from 150 years of breeding that selected traits of intelligence, gentleness, and affection. So despite being intended as gundogs, golden retrievers more often end up as family pets, as our Ben has.

Living in such close relationship with human beings means that domestic animals have become dependent on us and, as a result, vulnerable. We feed and care for them, and they depend on us. Our Ben looks to us for affection, attention, and even instruction. In a word, he is tamed.

If the relationship between animals and humans helps us understand why Jesus was laid in a manger, it also gives us insight to the presence of the shepherds in the story.

Remember that authors actively choose plot, characters, and settings. They select specific details to communicate specific realities. The same is true of the Christmas story. As its author, God set up the plot, pacing, and actors of the drama. So when I read that he sends his angels to shepherds and not to farmers, fishermen, or Pharisees, I can't help but wonder, *Why? Why shepherds?*

One possible answer lies in the message that comes to the shepherds. In the middle of the night as they are keeping watch, the angel of the Lord appears before them in a blaze of glory. "Don't be afraid," he comforts these terrified guardians, "for look, I proclaim to you good news of great joy that will be for all the people: Today in the city of David a Savior was born for you, who is the Messiah, the Lord."[1]

"The city of David" is none other than Bethlehem, a town in the "same region" where a newly born baby lay sleeping in swaddling bands. While Bethlehem is the setting of the story of Ruth and Boaz, its primary significance was as the birthplace of their great-grandson, David—the shepherd of flocks who became the shepherd of God's people. So tied is Bethlehem to Israel's royal line that Micah prophesies that the Promised Son will also be born in Bethlehem. But Micah also adds another interesting detail. Speaking of the Promised Son, he writes:

> His origin is from antiquity,
> from ancient times.
> Therefore, Israel will be abandoned until the
>     time
> when she who is in labor has given birth. . . .
> He will stand and shepherd them
> in the strength of the LORD,
> in the majestic name of the LORD his God.

> They will live securely,
> for then his greatness will extend
> to the ends of the earth.[2]

Supreme artist that he is, God is not about to miss an opportunity for symbolism. So when his Shepherd is finally born, he sends the news to . . . shepherds. Who better to proclaim that David's heir has arrived than those who keep watch in the fields as he once did? Who better to understand the significance of a leader who will protect and care for his people than those who are doing the same for their flock?

Later during his earthly ministry, Jesus declares himself to be the Good Shepherd that Micah prophesied about:

> I know my own, and my own know me, just as the Father knows me, and I know the Father. I lay down my life for the sheep. But I have other sheep that are not from this sheep pen; I must bring them also, and they will listen to my voice. Then there will be one flock, one shepherd.[3]

And suddenly the angels' words become clear: these *are* tidings of great joy which will be for all people. Jesus will shepherd a flock greater than David ever did. His care will extend far beyond Bethlehem to the ends of the earth. And indeed, every day he is adding to this flock, bringing people from every tribe, tongue, and nation together under his protection.

But the Promised Son is more than a strong shepherd with a large flock. He is also a *Good* Shepherd, the kind of shepherd who stands between his flock and destruction and offers himself as a sacrifice. And not only does this Good Shepherd protect his sheep, he also does not harm them. He does not abuse them. He does not take advantage of their dependence on him.

Lest you think I'm stating the obvious, consider the risks that come with being domesticated. When an animal is tamed—when it learns to listen to its master's voice—it lets down its guard. It begins to trust. It becomes vulnerable. Under a good master, this openness is beautiful because it allows the master to come close enough to care for an animal. This is especially important when an animal is hurt, afraid, or malnourished. But in submitting to a master, the animal also opens itself to the possibility of harm.

In this moment of vulnerability, cruel and selfish owners can take advantage of an animal's lack of natural guardedness; and far too often, domesticated animals suffer precisely *because* they've been domesticated. Whether it manifests in neglect or blood sport, such cruelty is especially perverse because it takes advantage of the trust an animal places in us.

So too, when earthly leaders abuse their role in our lives, they take advantage of our vulnerability. They take advantage of the fact that we've let down our guard and allowed them to come close. Good leaders understand and honor this trust, humbly using it to better care for us. But immature and evil leaders misuse it for their own ends. And ultimately, their cruelty is expressed in falsehood, manipulation, and predatory behaviors—behaviors which will be magnified a hundred times across the breadth of churches, workplaces, and nations. This is why Proverbs says that "when the righteous are in authority, the people rejoice; But when a wicked man rules, the people groan."[4] It's also why God promises to hold such leaders to account himself.

In Jeremiah 23, the Lord declares: "Woe to the shepherds who destroy and scatter the sheep of my pasture! . . . You have scattered my flock, banished them, and have not attended to them. I am about to attend to you because of your evil acts."[5]

But because justice alone is not enough, God also promises to heal us when we have been abused. He promises to regather his flock and return us to places of safety and flourishing. He promises that we "will no longer be afraid or discouraged, nor will any be missing."[6] And to prove it, he promises us the Good Shepherd:

> "Look, the days are coming"—this is the
> LORD's declaration—
> "when I will raise up a Righteous Branch for
> David.
> He will reign wisely as king
> and administer justice and righteousness in
> the land."
> In his days Judah will be saved,
> and Israel will dwell securely."[7]

Yes, the Good Shepherd lays his life down for his flock, but he also cares for us when we have been harmed, when our trust is broken and our vulnerability exploited. And just as he himself was raised to new life, he promises to raise us as well.

Hear this truth: the Lord is your Good Shepherd. He calls you to himself. And as you follow his voice, he will lead you beside still waters. He will restore your soul. When you walk through the darkest valleys and your fears come pressing in, when the pain and memories surface, he will be with you protecting, defending, and comforting you. He will supply all you need and guard you when those who hate you come near. He will fill your days with goodness and mercy until he brings you safely home to dwell in his house forever.

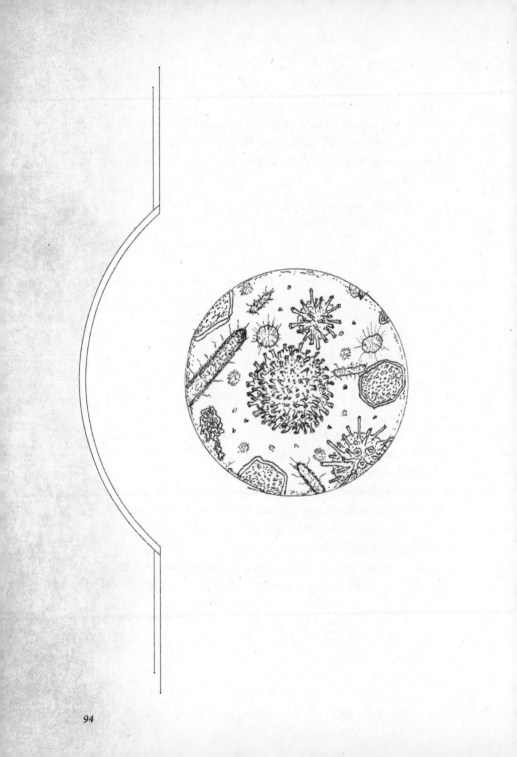

# 16

# Visible and Invisible

There's nothing like a global pandemic to make us all experts in microbiology. Over the last few years, I've learned more about germ theory, infectious spread, viral load, and gene mutation than I ever wanted to know. Not that I'm ungrateful for modern science. In the same years, our collective knowledge and the commitment of researchers and medical professionals have saved more lives than we'll ever know. But in the past, plagues had a more mysterious quality to them, at least from an experiential standpoint. The ancients had a sense of "little creatures" at the root of illness, but prevailing theories blamed epidemics on "bad air" or noxious vapors. Today we know that disease is spread by specific microorganisms like bacteria, fungi, and viruses—and we can't escape that knowledge even if we wanted to.

Invisible to the naked eye, these pathogens swarm and swirl all around us. They rest on countertops and doorknobs, travel by handshake and kiss, and can create a world of chaos if left unchecked. To be fair, not all mircoorganisms are bad. Good bacteria help digest food in our gut, fermenting yeasts give us bread and kombucha, and don't look now, but your skin is a miniature ecosystem, teeming with life.

Of course, we wouldn't know any of this if it weren't for the invention of the microscope. Sometime in the thirteenth century, inventors began to experiment more seriously with the principles of magnification and lens crafting, and soon enough they'd made instruments that allowed them to the see things both up close and far away. While Johannes Kepler and Galileo Galilei pointed their lenses toward the planets, others, like Robert Hooke and Anton van Leeuwenhoek, turned their lenses to worlds closer to home.

Beginning with the cellular structures of plants and animals, scientists soon discovered an entire world of organisms so small they had been undetectable, and thus unknown, by humans. The irony, of course, is that these "germs" existed long before the microscope was invented and did not suddenly become real just because scientists could now see them. Just as distant stars burn with or without our permission, germs reproduce, spread, and harm whether we see and acknowledge them or not. What changed with the invention of the microscope was our ability to see what had always been there. What changed was our perception.

Because of this, the microscope changed us at deeper levels, too. What Winston Churchill said is true: "We shape our tools and then the tools shape us." Now able to see organisms once invisible, we began to see other things differently as well. We began to believe that what we *can* see is all there is to see. What before had been mysterious is now traceable, identifiable, and quantifiable. And satisfied with this knowledge, we're less comfortable with the unknown. I think about this when I read Luke's account of the angels who appear before the shepherds in the fields.

> Then an angel of the Lord stood before them,
> and the glory of the Lord shone around them,
> and they were terrified. But the angel said to
> them, "Don't be afraid, for look, I proclaim
> to you good news of great joy that will be for
> all the people: Today in the city of David a
> Savior was born for you, who is the Messiah,

the Lord. This will be the sign for you: You will find a baby wrapped tightly in cloth and lying in a manger."

Suddenly there was a multitude of the heavenly host with the angel, praising God and saying: Glory to God in the highest heaven, and peace on earth to people he favors![1]

This isn't the first time angels have shown up in the Christmas story. Gabriel appeared to Zechariah in the temple. Joseph saw an angel in a dream, and Mary herself was also visited by Gabriel. At this point angels seem to be everywhere.

But it makes you wonder: maybe they are.

Just as microorganisms did not suddenly come into existence with the invention of the microscope, these heavenly beings did not come into existence when the shepherds saw them. Nor did they come from some faraway galaxy as a kind of intergalactic space invader. What changed in this moment was the shepherds' ability to perceive a world that was typically hidden from them. What changed was their ability to see the "visionary realm," as Paul calls the metaphysical world in the letter to the Colossians.[2]

What changed was that God, for a few moments, pulled back the curtain to reveal what had been there all along.

This doesn't detract from the miracle of it any more than our ability to see microscopic cells makes them less amazing. The presence of angels throughout the Christmas story signals that something unusual is happening. Because it is not any more normal to physically see angels singing the praises of God than it is to see the bacteria that live on your countertop with your naked eye. The miracle of this moment is not the angels themselves. It's that the angels *appeared*. The miracle is that metaphysical beings manifested in physical form so humans could perceive them.

The miracle is that a God who does not have a body just showed up in one.

And when such things happen, when the veil between this world and that one is pulled back for even a moment, the only proper response is exactly what the shepherds did. They looked at one another, and they decided to find out more, saying, "Let's go straight to Bethlehem and see what has happened, which the Lord has made known to us."[3] The only proper response to germ and angel alike is humble curiosity at what God has revealed.

Because when the curtain is pulled back, when the microscopic is enlarged, it looks nothing like anything you've ever seen before. Read Ezekiel's description of the seraphim that surround the throne of God or John's in Revelation, and you'd be forgiven if you confuse them for the living creatures on the specimen slide. And don't think for one minute that you could handle knowing all there is to know about the microorganisms swarming and swirling around you right now. Perhaps it's a grace that we can't see either angels or germs. Perhaps it's more than our senses can bear, more than they were ever meant to bear.

I don't profess to understand the spiritual realm, nor am I attempting to teach a systematic theology of angels, but I do know that they are part of the universe God has made. And I do know that

> when he brings his firstborn into the world,
> he says,
> And let all God's angels worship him.
> And about the angels he says:
> He makes his angels winds,
> and his servants a fiery flame.[4]

And just because we cannot see, smell, taste, hear, or touch something does not mean that it does not exist or that the world around us is not right now pulsating with *invisibilia.*

Reality is not bound by human senses. The limits of our physical bodies are no standard for what is true and what is not. If germ theory and the appearance of angels teach us anything, it's that the world is both much smaller and much grander than we currently know. It is full of mystery and wonder, of things seen and things yet unseen.

But this is a little thing for those who follow a God who took on flesh. It is a little thing for those who live between what is and what will be—who live believing that certain realities are true even as we cannot yet see them to be true.

But occasionally, on starry nights, in unexpected and unpredictable ways, the curtain slips; and if only for a few moments, the invisible is revealed. In these moments, the only proper response is wonder and awe and the kind of fear that's permeated by delight and curiosity. Because if we're honest, we have to admit that this world is too much. Our minds cannot contain it any more than our hearts can. And so instead of trusting in our knowledge, we surrender to the mystery and the joy of it all—to the *God* of it all, who sees it all and knows it all and understands it all when we can't. We surrender, waiting for the glory of the Lord himself to be revealed.

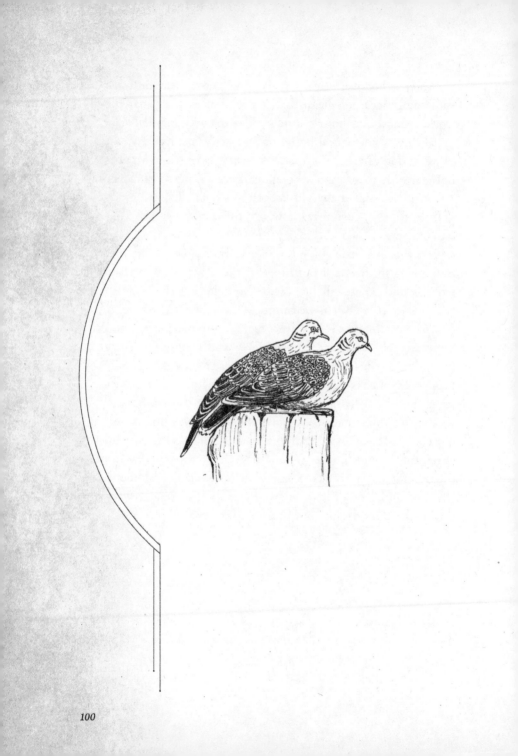

# 17

# Birds and Bees

I don't remember when I first learned where babies come from, but I do remember watching kittens be born before I was old enough for kindergarten. My grandmother's cat, a pretty calico named Bluebell, had found her way into the house and hidden in a box of paperwork under the bed. By the time we found her, she was halfway through a new litter. Later, my grandma showed me how to tell the difference between male and female by lifting their tails and looking between their legs.

I also watched Ginger, our brown Nubian nanny goat, birth twins on a Sunday evening. I remember it was a Sunday because we didn't go to Bible study, and to this day, I can picture her laboring in her cordwood shed. The black kid slipped out first followed by a brown one who matched his mother. Later, after they'd weaned, my dad showed me the mechanics of hand milking, how to grip her teat and squeeze my fingers to fill a bucket. Flocks of chickens taught me about ovaries and eggs, even if we did occasionally crack open a fertilized one while baking. Working in the garden meant finding Japanese beetles locked in coitus, and when we brought fish home from the lake, filleting them offered another lesson in biological differentiation.

The wonderful thing about growing up this way is that basic bodily processes like sex and birth were assumed to be normal long before they had a chance to be shamed or perverted. I'm especially grateful for this because it prepared me to read the Bible with the same matter-of-fact perspective as it is written. Scripture assumes a level of knowledge and comfort with how the world works and how each of us came into being, and that's nowhere clearer than in the Christmas story itself.

Sometime after the shepherds' visit, the Scripture records that Joseph and Mary took Jesus "up to Jerusalem to present him to the Lord" in keeping with the command to dedicate the firstborn son and to "offer a sacrifice (according to what is stated in the law of the Lord, a pair of turtledoves or two young pigeons)."[1] Reading quickly, you might think these refer to one event, but according to Numbers 18:14–16, the redemption price for a month-old male child was five shekels of silver, not two birds.

So, who was the sacrifice for? It was for Mary.

The law stipulated that when a woman gave birth, she would enter a period of "purification" during which she would be considered ceremonially unclean or *niddah*. According to Leviticus 12, when she gave birth to a son, this period would encompass two events. The first was the child's circumcision, which would occur eight days into her purification.

While fairly common in the United States, circumcision in the Greco-Roman world was a particular feature of Jewish life that wasn't shared by their surrounding culture. Advocates today offer medical and hygienic reasons to remove the foreskin of an infant's penis, but for first-century Jews, it was a theological and sociological practice, one that identified them with Yahweh and one another.[2] Strangely to us, circumcision was a public celebration that included naming the child. Jesus would likely have been circumcised and named in Bethlehem, surrounded by friends and family including Zechariah, Elizabeth, and John who had been circumcised and named a few months earlier (an event Mary likely attended herself).

After the circumcision, the mother would continue another thirty-three days in *niddah* until her own purification. At the end, she would bring a burnt offering to the temple, and the priest would make atonement for her. Before the offering though, Leviticus 12 warns that "she must not touch any holy thing or go into the sanctuary until completing her days of purification."[3]

If you weren't already feeling uncomfortable, you probably are now. Because in our modern way of thinking, this sounds like Mary was somehow defiled by birth—that she carried a kind of guilt or filth from what was an entirely natural process, a process God had created and, in this case, was more than directly responsible for. And indeed, some will read guilt into these purification rituals. So inherently sinful are we, the reasoning goes, that even our bodies are existentially impure. Whether it was a woman who was *niddah* after giving birth or a man who was the same after a seminal ejaculation, our flesh, they say, is sinful by its very nature and must be redeemed by a sin offering.

But while it's true that the effects of sin reach farther than any of us understand, the point of these rituals is actually not to shame the body or show our flesh to be inherently sinful. In fact, these purification rituals teach the exact opposite. They teach that God affirms and values our bodies, perhaps even more than we do. God affirms and values our bodies so much that he is not content with merely a spiritual relationship; he wants us both body and soul.

To understand how purification honors the body, remember that a thing or a place is made sacred by differentiating it from the mundane world around it. When the Jews rededicated the temple, they set it apart for the worship of a God who was unlike anything else in his creation. Common things had to be made uncommon, not because they were inherently sinful but because they were being sanctified to his service. Remember, ordinary olive oil, a wonderful and good gift from God that was useful for all kinds of things, only became holy, anointing oil when it was set apart. It was *made* holy by dedicating it to God. So, too, our bodies are wonderful, good gifts from God to be received with gratitude and joy for all the things they do and allow us to do. But God is so different from our bodies. He is so far beyond our earthy, material existence that in order to commune with him *in these bodies*, they, too, must be set apart for him, if only for a time.

Instead of signaling God's distaste for our bodies, these rituals imply a deep love for them. This love is why the Bible often feels so earthy and so much more comfortable than we are with topics like sex, reproduction, and bodily functions. It's why God doesn't shy away from commanding Jewish boys to be circumcised and Jewish mothers to go through the process of ritual purification. Rather than condemning our bodies, God is essentially saying, "I want all of you, right down to those parts you consider private. Right down to those parts you've been taught to detest, shame, or take for granted. I want you to understand that your whole self is being set apart for me. And this goes not only for the newest little lives but the life-givers too."

In fact, so much does God value our bodies that he made provision for all people, regardless of resources or background, to be able to sanctify their bodies before him. Because while Mary brought two doves to sacrifice, this was actually a concession made for the poor who could not afford the year-old male lamb and a young pigeon the law actually required.[4] As wild and as common as human bodies themselves, the sacrifice of these birds captures both the vulnerability and ubiquity of our physical existence.

And nobody would have known that better, or felt it more deeply, than a poor, young woman who'd just given birth. A woman whose body is stretched and marked, tired and sagging. A body that she herself may not recognize at this point. A body she herself may not love. By giving her the option to sacrifice these birds when she could afford nothing greater, God communicates that he wants nothing to stand in the way of her ability to commune with him in her body.

And suddenly I understand a bit more of Jesus's anger in Matthew 21 when he enters the temple just days before his crucifixion. I understand why he overturned the tables of the money changers and "the chairs of those selling doves."[5] I understand why he wouldn't let anything stand in the way of those coming to commune with God in prayer, wanting to worship him in bodies sanctified, accepted, and made whole.

When I think about the incarnation, with all its earthiness and all its mystery, when I think how God came in a body to sanctify our bodies, I can't help but rejoice. And on the days when I feel especially broken, defiled, and earthbound, I hear the words of the apostle Paul anew: "But you were washed, you were sanctified, you were justified in the name of the Lord Jesus Christ and by the Spirit of our God. . . . Your body is a temple of the Holy Spirit who is in you, whom you have from God?"[6]

And instead of condemnation, there is acceptance. Instead of commonness, there is sacredness. And in this acceptance, I rejoice with the joy of one who is known, both body and soul.

# 18

# Boughs of Holly

The house we eventually bought when we moved back to Virginia is a 1960 brick ranch. Neat and trim, it testifies to all we know to be true about the community around it. Its hardwood floors, copper pipes, and eat-in kitchen are unpretentious, sensible, and built to last. This aesthetic also explains the presence of the six holly bushes once planted along its front. Because holly is evergreen and fairly low maintenance, it is a good, practical choice for landscapes and gardens, especially for people whose lives are too busy to tend fussier ornamentals. But holly's delicate white flowers produce a significant amount of pollen just when you want to throw the doors and windows open. Their location so close to the house combined with our youngest son's extreme springtime allergies meant that these bushes had to go.

This was easier said than done. At first, Nathan tried to dig them out, but their extensive root system kept them firmly planted. Undeterred, he opted for force, wrapping a chain around the base of one and attaching it to the bumper of his truck. One bent bumper later, it was obvious who was winning. Eventually, he recruited help in the form of a passing neighbor with a bigger truck, and soon enough, the additional torque and horsepower ripped the bushes from the earth.

You'd think we'd finally won. And yet a decade later, we're still pulling up shoots from the taproots that were left behind.

Holly's perseverance, both as an evergreen and a deeply rooted shrub, is misrepresented by the neat, domesticated versions we often find in neighborhood landscaping. In the wild, some varieties of holly grow up to eighty feet tall and forty feet wide, making it more like a tree than a bush. The ancients saw this as a sign of nature's endurance and a promise that spring would return. The Romans incorporated holly into their worship of Saturn, and the Druids believed it warded off evil spirits. Eventually, it became a mainstay of Christian tradition, especially during the seasons of Advent and Christmas when its glossy leaves and bright red berries were used to "deck the halls." In fact, medieval church accounts record holly being used in church decorations from at least the twelfth century.[1] But holly was more than a convenient seasonal decoration.

For the early and medieval church, the natural world held spiritual mysteries within itself, standing as a kind of physical manifestation of truth. Holly was a shrub, but it was more than that. This may seem a bit too mystical for us in the modern West, but don't forget that we live in a world of universal and compulsory education focused almost exclusively on the development of the mind. From our earliest days, we're taught the meaning behind the letters and numbers on a page. But imagine a time in which books do not exist—or at the very least, they are the purview of the wealthy and powerful. In such a world, learning to decode the meaning behind a collection of letters would be far less useful than learning to decode the meaning behind the natural world around you. This did not mean people were unintelligent, merely that their shared knowledge base was different from ours. And so for generations of Christians before us, natural revelation was the means of communicating spiritual truth.

I think about this—how God's work is not bound by education or class—when I read about Simeon in Luke 2:25. Introduced to us simply as "a man in Jerusalem," the most important thing about Simeon is that he is "righteous and devout, looking forward to Israel's consolation, and the Holy Spirit was on him."[2] His presence in the temple might lead you to think he was part of the priesthood like Zechariah, but nothing in the passage suggests this. He's in the temple on the day Mary and Joseph came to complete "everything according to the law of the Lord,"[3] because the Spirit had led him there.

Having been promised by God that he would not die until he saw the coming Son, Simeon is by now an elderly man, longing deeply for the world to be made right. When he sees the infant Jesus, he is overcome with joy, sweeping him up in his arms in an unaffected gesture of pure delight. Then this ordinary man proclaims:

> Now, Master,
> you can dismiss your servant in peace,
> as you promised.
> For my eyes have seen your salvation.
> You have prepared it
> in the presence of all peoples—
> a light for revelation to the Gentiles
> and glory to your people Israel.[4]

But Simeon has something else he needs to say. Maybe it was the years of living in the brokenness, the decades of waiting and longing, the wisdom that can only be learned from hard times and hopes crushed a hundred times over, but he knows redemption will not come easily. He knows there is no life without pain, no salvation without suffering. So he turns to Mary with these words:

> Indeed, this child is destined to cause the fall
> and rise of many in Israel and to be a sign
> that will be opposed—and a sword will pierce

your own soul—that the thoughts of many
hearts may be revealed.[5]

Scholars interpret these words as prophesying the coming
crucifixion and passion of Jesus. And in this sense, they are
deeply theological and deeply Christian. Because while the
Romans and Druids celebrated holly as a symbol of persevering life, Christians saw something darker hidden among
those thorny leaves and red berries. They saw something of
its piercing nature. They saw in it a crown of thorns, spilled
blood, and life *after* death. Known in some languages as
"Christ thorn," holly became for them a symbol of Christ's
suffering for the world.

Because one day, the thorns of Genesis 3, the ones that
grow up from the cursed ground, would press into the head
of the promised Son. They would bite and tear at his flesh,
piercing his brow, the sins of the world mocking him. This
was the life he was born to, the life he was destined for—to
be a Savior for the oppressed, a light to the Gentiles, and a
Suffering Servant.

It was also the life Mary was called to share with him, to
walk out her faith, not just in the moment of his birth but
over the years of his life. Refusing to protect him from his
calling and, instead, supporting and participating in it—from
his first miracle at the wedding feast to the foot of the cross
and the empty tomb. Mary was called to carry the weight of a
mother's heart pierced by her Son's suffering.

Because just as shoots of holly keep popping up in my
front yard, the curse does not go easily. The thorns continue
to grow because sin's roots run deeper than any of us understand. Nothing short of the life and death of the Promised
Son can break its grip on this world.

Like Mary, we, too, are called into the suffering of Jesus. To bear witness with the world as it groans for redemption. To proclaim that the blood of the Savior is the only thing that can turn back the thorns. To know that if we follow in his steps, we will find our own hearts pierced as well.

"Dear friends," writes the apostle Peter, "don't be surprised when the fiery ordeal comes among you to test you, as if something unusual were happening to you. Instead, rejoice as you share in the sufferings of Christ, so that you may also rejoice with great joy when his glory is revealed."[6]

This is a strange kind of joy—one that cannot be explained by sentimentality or celebration. It's the joy of an old man like Simeon, exhausted and broken by the suffering of the world, holding hope in his arms. It is the joy of a mother like Mary knowing that her child will change everything, but that she will lose him in the process. It is the joy of those of us who have followed this Promised Son in the way of suffering and found him faithful.

It is the joy of the holly tree, the joy of sharp pain and glorious beauty persevering together.

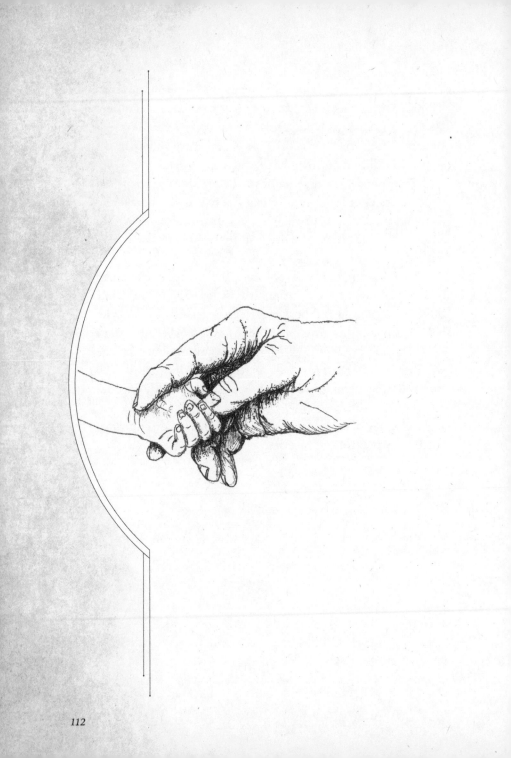

# 19

# Fullness of Time

Every Friday afternoon, a copy of *The Town Herald* lands in my mailbox. Somewhat miraculously in our age of media consolidation, *The Town Herald* has been in continuous publication since 1891, and each weekend I take full advantage of it. I'll scan the headlines ("Return of Christmas Parade Draws Crowds"), flip to the real estate listings (Terry's finally put his mother's house on the market), and read the personals ("Congratulations on your retirement, Loveda!"). Then after a quick read of high school sports and church notices, I'll allow myself to settle in with the obituaries. Because if I'm honest, I buy *The Town Herald* almost exclusively for the obituaries.

My family can tell you that this quirk is part of a larger fascination with aging and death. They can also tell you that I've already planned my funeral and that my most pressing perennial concern is not knowing where my body will be buried to await the resurrection. But lest you worry about me, I have no intention of passing any time soon. My maternal great-grandmother lived well into her nineties, and I've decided to do the same.

But nine decades is a lot of time to fill, and I want to make sure I do it well. So I read obituaries. I read them to figure out how Teresa Proffit became a woman whose grandchildren adored her and will be remembered for her homemade biscuits and gravy. I read them to understand how the Reverend James P. Hollins came to be so revered and why his funeral will draw mourners from six different states. I read them to know what made animals and children implicitly trust Leonard Smalley and how his marriage to Alice was a source of joy for fifty-three years. I read the obituaries to learn—not how to die but how to live.

Of course, the one challenge inherent in living like Mrs. Proffit and Reverend Hollins is growing old. Because as much as I want to make it to my nineties, I'm not sure I'm entirely comfortable with the process it takes to get there. Some of this is due to our cultural obsession with youth. Fifty is the new thirty, they tell you, but in my experience, no one professes it more loudly than those desperately trying to hold onto their thirties. So buy this eye cream, and here's a small blue pill, and you're only as old as you think you are.

But my discomfort with aging goes beyond cultural conditioning. In many ways, aging undermines everything I've learned to be true about living. For most of life, growing a year older meant greater physical strength and more independence. But now, instead of strengthening our bones, the years make them weaker. Instead of more knowledge, the years rob our minds of memories. We go through puberty in reverse. Our eyesight clouds, our hearing deteriorates, and we become more like children again, as our world shrinks to fit our new limitations.

So I find myself thinking a lot about death and aging, and perhaps this explains why I can't yet leave Luke's account of Mary and Joseph in the temple. After recording Simeon's words to Mary, Luke pivots to introduce us to Anna, a prophetess who spends her days serving God through fasting and prayer. Like Simeon, she is devout and looking for the Promised Son. Like Simeon, she is caught up in the joy of the moment, praising God and speaking about Jesus "to all who were looking forward to the redemption of Jerusalem."[1]

And like Simeon, she is "well along in years."[2]

To be fair, "well along in years" is a bit of an understatement. Widowed after only seven years of marriage, Anna has likely served in the temple since then; and while the Greek is a bit ambiguous, she is either eighty-four years old or has been widowed for eighty-four years, which would make her at least 105. So here in Luke 2 we have a woman who is possibly a centenarian alongside a man who is about to die—and *these* are the people God calls to testify to Jesus as the Redeemer. *Why them?*

Some theologians note that Simeon and Anna fulfill the law's standard for testimony to be established by two witnesses; and indeed, they both separately proclaim that this baby Jesus, newly dedicated to God, is the long Promised Son. In 2 Peter 1, the apostle writes about the importance of such prophetic words being "confirmed" saying that "no prophecy of Scripture comes from the prophet's own interpretation, because no prophecy ever came by the will of man; instead, men spoke from God as they were carried along by the Holy Spirit."[3] But he also emphasizes the importance of our paying attention to such words—especially those that proclaim Jesus as the Promised Son—because they are like "a lamp shining in a dark place, until the day dawns and the morning star rises in your hearts."[4]

Something about the kind of testimony Simeon and Anna offered up in the temple helps keep our hope alive. Something about their certain joy helps stir up our own, even while we wait for our faith to be proved true. And while the Scripture points to Anna's and Simeon's devotion, it's their age that catches my attention. In their old age, they represent more than their own faithfulness. They represent the faithfulness of generations who have gone before them. They testify on behalf of all those who have waited and longed for a promise that they never got to see.

In Hebrews 11, the author lists the names of Old Testament saints who "died in faith, although they had not received the things that were promised. But they saw them from a distance, greeted them, and confessed that they were foreigners and temporary residents on the earth."[5] It was precisely the temporariness of their lives that inspired their faith. They were people who knew they wouldn't be around forever, and this perspective changed how they lived out the time they did have. Peter tells us to pay attention to such testimony so we will be "able to recall these things at any time after [their] departure."[6]

And of all the things Peter needed to say before he passed, of all the things Simeon and Anna needed to express, it was the certainty of Jesus as a source of joy. As I think about this, it makes me wonder—perhaps sight doesn't diminish with age. Perhaps it focuses in on the things that are most important. Perhaps our ears don't grow deaf but simply attune to our Savior's voice. Perhaps by returning to a state of childlike dependence, we move closer to the kingdom than we've ever been.

And perhaps, just perhaps, we can leave a path for others to follow on this earth—even if we no longer walk it ourselves. As the author of Hebrews continues:

> All these were approved through their faith,
> but they did not receive what was promised,
> since God had provided something better for
> us, so that they would not be made perfect
> without us.
>
> Therefore, since we also have such a large
> cloud of witnesses surrounding us, let us lay
> aside every hindrance and the sin that so eas-
> ily ensnares us. Let us run with endurance

the race that lies before us, keeping our eyes
on Jesus.[7]

As witnesses to the faithfulness of God, those who have
gone before us encourage us to keep going and teach us to
focus on the joy that is waiting.

I can think of worse ways to grow old. I can think of worse
things to become than a woman who goes on and on and on
about the Promised Son and spends her days in prayer and
fasting. I can think of worse ways to be taken up into that
great cloud of witnesses.

So when my eyesight fades and my mind begins to wander, when my children take me by the hand and have hushed
conversations behind my back, I hope to be an old woman
whose joy is undiminished, who babbles on about beauty and
goodness and life. Who, though I lose my thoughts, never lose
my songs, and whose quavering voice continues to herald the
good news until her final breath: "Even while I am old and
gray, God, do not abandon me, while I proclaim your power
to another generation, your strength to all who are to come."[8]

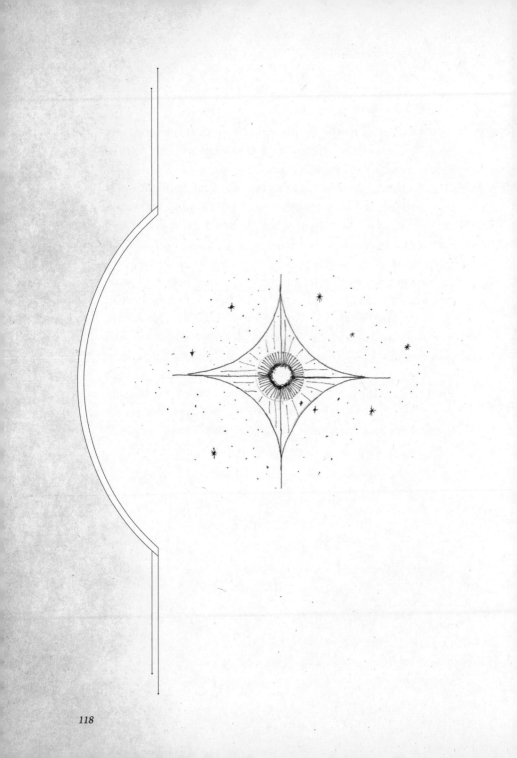

# 20

# Starry Night

The night sky is different in the country. I'm reminded of this as I step outside with my bucket of kitchen scraps and peer into the darkness. Winter solstice is closing in now, and the days grow increasingly shorter as the earth's axis reaches its fullest tilt away from the sun while it also reaches the furthest point on its orbit.[1] Even though it's still early, just after dinner, night has already descended in its fullness.

My breath curls and holds in the air as I slip on boots and head toward the garden. My nose and eyes water against the chill, and all around me is an encompassing darkness. In more populated areas, this darkness would be diminished by a phenomenon called sky glow in which the accumulation of artificial light reflects back into the night. But in the country—without the bright lights of car dealerships, airports, and stadiums—the sky is black, perforated only by the light of stars streaming from galaxies far away.

I dump the eggshells, bread crusts, and potato peels, leaving them to decompose with yesterday's scraps. Eventually we'll turn and till it all into the ground, but for now the work of breaking down is more than enough. Tonight is also a new moon, the phase of the lunar cycle when the moon sits between the earth and the sun and is nearly invisible to the naked eye. Over the course of the next few weeks, it will wax fuller, gradually increasing until it reaches complete exposure, and then it will slowly wane, losing a bit of light each night until it sits in full darkness again.

On moonless nights like tonight the stars are especially bright, and a kind of peace descends as they rise. I can just make out Venus on the horizon with Jupiter and Saturn arching above her. Polaris, the North Star, sits high in the sky while constellations begin their nightly rotation around it. Under such a sky, I understand why the psalmist says that "the heavens declare the glory of God, and the expanse proclaims the work of his hands."[2] And if only for a few minutes, I can feel the gap of time closing. I feel a kinship with all those who've lived under the same sky, centuries and millennia before me.

For most of history, humans have depended on the stars, trusting their predictable movements to guide our own. Here in the mountains, there are still folks who plant by the signs—who put in their gardens when the moon sits at a certain position in the sky. And others can teach you how to find your way through the woods and ridges by orienting yourself to the North Star.

Because even though we are the ones turning, even though the earth is rotating on its axis while it orbits around the sun, we experience the stars as moving. In tracking their patterns across the heavens, we've learned how to determine where we sit on this vast globe. Throughout time, this "celestial navigation" has allowed us to cross oceans, establish trade routes, lead military campaigns, and even run to freedom. And in a completely unexpected twist, this celestial navigation also leads seekers to the Promised Son.

In Matthew 2, the apostle picks up the account of Jesus's birth by introducing us to "wise men from the east."[3] While Luke does not include this story in his retelling, some scholars place it shortly after the holy family's visit to the temple and their eventual return to Nazareth.[4] After detailing Jesus's royal lineage and the virgin birth, Matthew writes, "After Jesus was born in Bethlehem of Judea in the days of King

Herod, wise men from the east arrived in Jerusalem, saying, 'Where is he who has been born king of the Jews? For we saw his star at its rising and have come to worship him.'"[5]

The Greek word for "wise men" is *magi*, a term rich in meaning and allusion. Likely coming from Babylon or modern-day Iraq, these magi were powerful political and social leaders, who gained influence not through birth or military conquest but through their wisdom and knowledge. They were advisers to kings, and in fact, the Greek translation of the Old Testament names Daniel as among the "magi" in the Babylonian court. Eventually, Daniel's own ability to interpret dreams and offer counsel led to his elevation as second in command.

Much like the granny women of Appalachia who can tell you when to plant and what herbs cure a chest cold, these magi were revered for their knowledge of the natural world and their ability to interpret its meaning. In our modern age, we don't quite have an equivalent to the magi because we tend to separate politics, science, religion, and philosophy from one another. But the magi possessed the skills both to track celestial bodies and to interpret their significance. They would have had knowledge of history and sacred texts as well as science and mathematics. So, when they saw a new star rising, they took note and moved toward it.

Today, scholars think the star that led the magi to Jerusalem (and eventually Bethlehem) was a comet.[6] But this was no shooting star. Like the famed Halley's Comet, it would have gradually traveled across the sky over the course of several months, shifting relative position each night. Using star charts and the latest technology (like the astrolabe), the magi set out on a kind of scientific expedition, chasing the star wherever it led them. But they were also engaging in a religious pursuit, understanding that whoever was behind this spectacle was worthy of their worship.

And so those who carried off Daniel to serve among the magi in their homeland, now send their magi to Daniel's homeland to worship his God and true King. And just as the birth of the Good Shepherd was fittingly announced to shepherds, the birth of One who displays the wisdom and glory of God is fittingly announced by a glorious star. Isaiah foretells all this in Isaiah 60 when he writes:

> Arise, shine, for your light has come,
> and the glory of the LORD shines over you.
> For look, darkness will cover the earth,
> and total darkness the peoples;
> but the LORD will shine over you,
> and his glory will appear over you.
> Nations will come to your light,
> and kings to your shining brightness.
> Raise your eyes and look around:
> they all gather and come to you;
> your sons will come from far away.[7]

In the wisdom of God, the Promised Son becomes the star around which all the earth and heavens rotate. The Promised Son becomes a source of light and glory for the nations. And all anyone must do is follow the Star wherever he leads.

But such a journey can only begin with humility. It begins when wise men understand that they are not wise enough. It begins when pride is replaced with wonder and curiosity and a willingness to discover what we do not yet know. Because ultimately, worshipping the One revealed as "the way, the truth, and the life"[8] requires that we give up our own notions of truth and life. It requires that we enter a narrow way—one that is only accessible to those who do not rely on their own understanding and, instead, trust God to make the path straight before them.

During his earthly ministry, Jesus rebukes those who are confident in their own understanding and goodness. He says that the narrow door will be closed to them even as it opens to others.

> There will be weeping and gnashing of teeth in that place, when you see Abraham, Isaac, Jacob, and all the prophets in the kingdom of God, but yourselves thrown out. They will come from east and west, from north and south, to share the banquet in the kingdom of God.[9]

In the magi we find a witness to the honest pursuit of God. Rather than using their knowledge for personal advancement or political gain, they humbly seek the glory of the One the stars praise. They follow the light they have, and ultimately it leads them to a Baby. A Baby they are not too proud to fall down and worship. A Baby who himself is the light of the world.

We must walk in this same humility. If we are to walk in his light, we must acknowledge that he—and not ourselves—is the source of that light. So that whatever insight we've been granted, whatever path God's glory has led us down, we use this light to light the way for others. As the Hebrew magi himself writes: "Those who have insight will shine like the bright expanse of the heavens, and those who lead many to righteousness, like the stars forever and ever."[10]

Until that day when people from every tribe, tongue, and nation are gathered into the city of God, and the nations walk in his light forever.

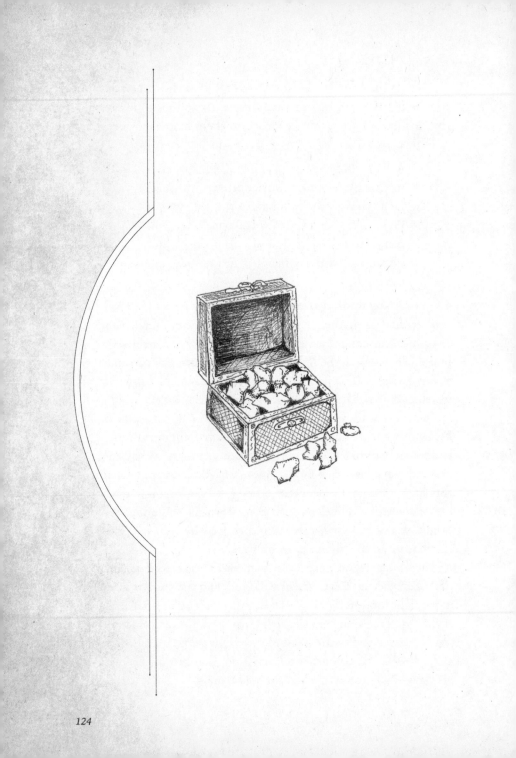

# 21

# Gold

When people think of Appalachia, they can't help but think of coal. For over 150 years, coal mining and its supporting industries have shaped its landscape, culture, and history. But coal is not the only mineral that lies beneath these hills, and before large-scale mining took hold, picks and shovels harvested iron ore, saltpeter, copper, and quartz.

So much so that when you're out hiking, it's not uncommon to come across abandoned mines. And if you follow the Blue Ridge down to the western Carolinas and Georgia, you'll find a heritage of mining more precious natural resources. In fact, gold was first discovered in the New World not in California, but in the central foothills of North Carolina. In 1799, an unsuspecting twelve-year-old boy picked up a shining seventeen-pound rock out of the creek on his family farm and took it home. Not knowing its value, his family used it as a doorstop for several years before they had it appraised.

Nearly three decades later, gold was also found in the mountains of north Georgia on land that belonged to the Cherokee Nation. White settlers soon rushed in to claim it while new state laws made it illegal for Cherokee to dig for gold on their own land. In 1830, Congress passed the Indian Removal Act, which provided the legal apparatus to drive tens of thousands of indigenous people from their ancestral lands and eventually led to the Trail of Tears. Forced to march west under brutal conditions, thousands of Cherokee died along the way—all because of a lust for gold.

If you learn anything from living in the mountains, it's that natural history predicts political history.

Throughout time and around the globe, war and oppression often find their roots in the struggle to control land and natural resources. The same was true of the world into which Jesus was born. At the time of his birth in Palestine, the Roman Empire was enjoying a period of relative stability historians know as the *Pax Romana* or the "peace of Rome." With major conflicts past, Rome maintained its reign by force, taxing the peoples they'd conquered and skimming natural resources for their temples, palaces, and lavish lifestyles.

But Rome was a geographically vast empire, so to ensure local obedience, they set up puppet kings to enforce this "peace." Herod was one such king. A vassal of Rome, his job was to maintain the status quo by farming the taxes and resources Rome expected from its conquered occupants. Beyond this, Herod was free to reign as he pleased, and historians mark his reign as both powerful and tyrannical. While he supported the Jews by renovating and expanding the temple, he was also deeply suspicious of anyone or anything, whether real or imagined, that might threaten his authority.

So when the magi show up in Jerusalem looking for the one who is "born king of the Jews,"[1] Herod is more than a little unsettled.

Calling for the chief priests and scribes, he asks them where the Promised Son would be born. "In Bethlehem," they tell him. Bethlehem. That town just a few miles down the road from where he sat. Bethlehem.

Keeping his cards close to his chest, Herod sends the magi to follow the star's movement, claiming that he, too, wants to worship the Promised Son. The magi continue on and eventually come to a house in Bethlehem where they find Jesus with his mother. Falling to their knees, they worship him and present their gifts: gold, frankincense, and myrrh.

To understand the significance of the magi's gifts, you must remember how often the treasures of Israel had been stripped from them, how often their temple vessels and palace storehouses had been plundered. How often they'd been conquered, controlled, and coerced into offering loyalty and homage to oppressive rulers. How often their own children and heirs had been carried to faraway lands to serve the needs of foreign empires.

You must also remember that God promised to return and restore what was lost through his Promised Son.

Having prophesied in Isaiah 60 that the "nations will come to your light, and kings to your shining brightness," Isaiah continues:

> The wealth of the nations will come to you.
> Caravans of camels will cover your land—
> young camels of Midian and Ephah—
> all of them will come from Sheba.
> They will carry gold and frankincense
> and proclaim the praises of the LORD.[2]

So in this moment, when magi from the east bow before the "one who is born king of the Jews" and return their treasures to him, the circle comes full circle. Whether they know it or not, they play a part in fulfilling God's promise. Whether they know it or not, they represent the nations bringing their gifts of gold and frankincense back to Israel's rightful heir. They represent all those who, like Daniel, had been stolen from their homeland and forced to serve in Babylon's courts. They represent a kingdom that is yet to come.

Because in a time when loyalty is enforced by the sword, these wise men bow of their own volition. In a time when taxes are compelled, the magi offer up their gifts freely. And by offering them up this way, they challenge everything that Rome and Herod stand for, testifying that the Promised Son is a truer, better King than any human empire could ever offer.

Because while earthly kings engage in constant battle for control and enforce a kind of peace, it is not a righteous peace. Indeed, even in this moment, Herod is plotting not for peace but for destruction, his lust for power and control corrupting everything he does. But just as gold itself does not tarnish or corrupt, the reign of the Prince of peace will also be pure and righteous. He will bring peace, not through political power and wealth-slinging but by his goodness. He will reign through sacrifice, and his love for the world will be so great that people all around the earth come to him freely in worship. And the magi are among the firstfruits of this coming kingdom. When they present gold to the baby Jesus, they testify that he, and not Herod, is the true King of the Jews. The true King of the world.

Later in Matthew's Gospel, Jesus declares his authority over all the earth and sends his emissaries into the world to proclaim his good and glorious kingdom.[3] But make no mistake, his kingdom threatens all earthly kingdoms because those who sit high on their thrones of power do not want to be toppled from them. And so we are not surprised when earthly kingdoms resist all that is good and true about the Promised Son. We are not surprised when they, like Herod, are "deeply disturbed"[4] by his presence.

But no other king is so good, so righteous, so kind, so just that he can command loyalty so freely. To no other king do the magi fall on their knees and offer up their treasures uncoerced. So we will also not be surprised when one day people from every tribe and tongue and nation freely offer up their praise as well. We will not be surprised when "every knee will bow—in heaven and on earth and under the earth—and every tongue will confess that Jesus Christ is Lord, to the glory of God the Father."[5]

In Revelation, John sees a vision of that final day when the Promised Son reigns as King. He sees a main street of "pure gold, transparent as glass." The glory of God illuminates the kingdom, and

> the nations will walk by its light, and the kings of the earth will bring their glory into it. . . . They will bring the glory and honor of the nations into it.[6]

And on that day, the nations will finally and truly be at peace—not through the false peace of empire but through the peace that comes when we all bow before the King of the earth. Because when rightly aligned to him, we will find ourselves aligned to one another. And with the magi of so long ago, we will join in a constellation of praise to our true and rightful King.

# 22

# Frankincense

We're just days from Christmas now, and the house is filled with the smells of the season. Sugar cookies cool on a rack near the oven. We've made the peanut butter fudge, and I'm mixing up cinnamon-brown sugar for sweet rolls. Wood smoke wafts up from the stove in the basement, and behind it all, holding strong is a curtain of fresh pine.

I catch a whiff of its earthy scent and remember that I need to water the tree, so I take a quart jar from the cupboard, fill it at the tap, and head to the living room. Crouching down, I push aside some gifts and extend my body as far under the lowest limbs as possible. The tree was well shaped to begin with, but we had to cut several bottom branches to make room for the skirt, and I can only just fit. I empty the water into the stand and do my best to emerge from the tree before rising, but I inevitably miscalculate and catch myself among its branches. My arm brushes against the trunk, and as always, I come up covered in sap.

Technically speaking, the substance on my fingers, face, and hair is *resin*, a fluid that some trees produce to close wounds and ward off disease. Pine resin is also known as *tar* or *pitch* and, when distilled, produces turpentine. It has antibacterial and anti-inflammatory properties, and if you've ever tried to scrub it off your skin, you also know that it is waterproof—which explains its historical use as a sealant. Sometimes if a wound on a pine tree is large enough and old enough, you might find hardened, jewel-like nodules of resin attached to the trunk. If you peel these crystals off and burn them, they'll release pine's distinctive aroma.

Interestingly, if you've experienced pine resin during the holidays, you also have a frame of reference for frankincense, the second gift the magi give to the Promised Son. Frankincense comes from the Boswellia tree of North Africa, Arabia, and India, which also produces resin to heal wounds and protect itself from disease. Like pine resin, it also has antimicrobial properties and hardens into small, jewel-like nodules. But unlike what's dripping from the tree in my living room, frankincense was and is exceptionally rare.

To stimulate production, cultivators intentionally wound the trunk of Boswellia trees and then collect the bits of hardened resin over time. In the first century, these "pearls of the desert" then traveled along trade routes by caravan. Revelation 18 even lists frankincense among the luxury items the merchants brought to Babylon: "cargo of gold, silver, jewels, and pearls; fine linen, purple, silk, and scarlet; all kinds of fragrant wood products; objects of ivory; objects of expensive wood, brass, iron, and marble; cinnamon, spice, incense, myrrh, and frankincense."[1]

Particularly prized for its sweet, woody aroma that releases when burned, frankincense was also a feature of temple worship. It was an ingredient in the holy anointing oil, was placed on the table of shewbread, and was burned on the altar of incense. In fact, Zechariah would have been burning frankincense (along with other spices) when Gabriel appeared to him in the sanctuary. And so if gold hints to the Promised Son's kingly role, frankincense hints to his priestly role. Because just as God was going to establish a true and lasting kingdom through Jesus, he was also going to establish true and lasting worship.

Remember that throughout Israel's history, the temple had been repeatedly defiled and ransacked. Holy vessels were carried off, and Daniel 5 even records that Belshazzar, a king of Babylon, used them as drinking glasses in a bacchanal (albeit one cut short by the famous handwriting on the wall). By the time of Jesus's birth, the original ark of the covenant with the stone tablets, Aaron's rod, and pot of manna had been lost.

Each time the temple was restored, new vessels were furnished and sanctified. Herod himself even expanded and updated the temple, but there was no escaping the fact that the temple was vulnerable and, despite its glory, temporary. Jesus calls attention to this during his earthly ministry when he foretells the temple's eventual and final destruction, saying that "not one stone will be left here on another that will not be thrown down."[2]

In this sense, the gift of frankincense foreshadows the unique relationship Jesus will have with the temple—one that both includes and transcends it.

This relationship begins in infancy when Jesus is first publicly recognized as the Promised Son in the temple. A few years later, the boy Jesus finds himself among the teachers of the temple, asking them questions and answering theirs. When his mother Mary chides him, he replies, "Didn't you know that it was necessary for me to be in my Father's house?"[3] Then throughout his life, Jesus regularly worships at the temple, fulfilling all the law requires. And just days before his crucifixion, he drives out the money changers and overturns the tables of the dove merchants proclaiming, "Is it not written, My house will be called a house of prayer for all nations? But you have made it a den of thieves!"[4]

Jesus's reference to the temple as a place of prayer is particularly striking when you remember that frankincense was burned during morning and evening prayers. As the smoke of sacrifice and incense ascended to heaven, so did the petitions of the people, rising as a sweet smell in the nostrils of God. But it's also significant that Jesus receives the gift of frankincense from foreigners. Isaiah 56—the passage he quotes while he is cleansing the temple—promises that God receives all who come to worship him, regardless of their national or ethnic origin:

> As for the foreigners who join themselves to
>     the LORD
> to minister to him, to love the name of the
>     LORD,
> and to become his servants—
> all who keep the Sabbath without
>     desecrating it
> and who hold firmly to my covenant—
> I will bring them to my holy mountain
> and let them rejoice in my house of prayer.
> Their burnt offerings and sacrifices
> will be acceptable on my altar,
> for my house will be called a house of prayer
> for all nations.[5]

And so it is fitting that the gift representing Jesus's priestly calling should be given by those who come from afar—by "foreigners who join themselves to the LORD . . . and become his servants."

These words hit me deeply when I remember my own family history. Even though I don't know my lineage in detail, I do know that my ancestors were not among the children of Israel. When the magi were bringing their gifts to the Promised Son, my ancestors were more than likely worshipping under the boughs of Odin's Oak. So the invitation for foreigners to worship the Lord and to have their prayers ascend to God is not lost on me. In fact, I would not be writing these words today had someone, somewhere, at some point not proclaimed the Promised Son as our High Priest as well.

Thinking of all this reminds me of Paul's words in 1 Timothy. Urging "that petitions, prayers, intercessions, and thanksgivings be made for everyone," he tells Timothy that God "wants everyone to be saved and to come to the knowledge of the truth. For there is one God and one mediator between God and mankind, the man Christ Jesus, who gave himself as a ransom for all."[6]

The Promised Son is the great High Priest between God and all humanity. And the work he began in the temple, to remove every barrier and restore it as a house of prayer, he continues to do to this day, opening a way for all people to come to the Father.

In Revelation 21, when John sees the streets of gold in the New Jerusalem where all the nations come, he also notes that there is no temple "because the Lord God the Almighty and the Lamb are its temple." The King who reigns is also our great High Priest, and his presence changes everything. John continues: "The city does not need the sun or the moon to shine on it, because the glory of God illuminates it, and its lamp is the Lamb. The nations will walk by its light."[7]

So today, we who were once far off can come boldly to our High Priest. We can come knowing that we are accepted, that no other sacrifice is needed other than his. We can come knowing that he sympathizes with our struggles and that his mercy and grace wait for us. So that despite all the chaos, both in and around us, we find peace, believing that our prayers are heard and that to him they are more precious than the sweet aroma of incense.

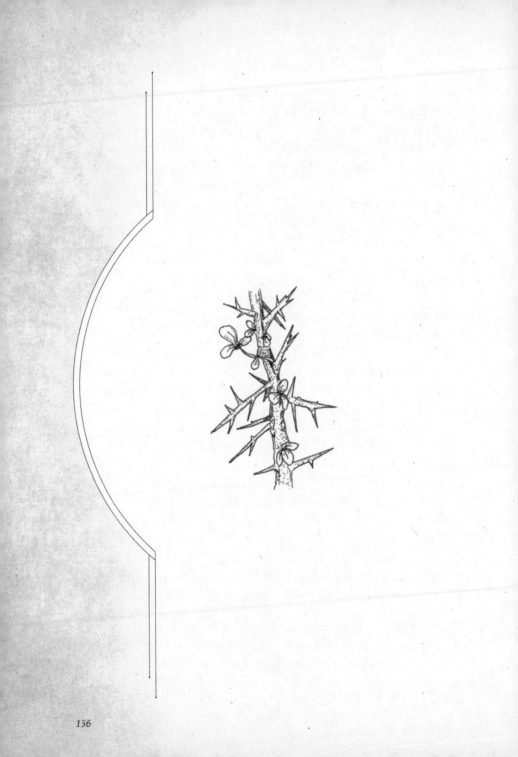

# 23

# Myrrh

O ne day closer to Christmas means one day further from being ready for Christmas. I still don't know how it happens. Every year, I'm always a present or two shy, behind in my gift wrapping, and rushing off to the grocery store for just one more thing. Having spent most of the day on my feet, I'm stealing a few minutes in front of the Christmas tree before bed. The only light in the room comes from between its needles, and I enjoy a rare moment of peace.

Seeing the boughs heavy with ornaments, I'm struck by how our Christmas tree has become more than a decoration, how it captures the different seasons of our family's life. There's the set of paper snowflakes I cut when we lived in New Zealand and Christmas came in the summer while I was desperate for home and winter. The personalized brass ornaments—one for each member of the family. The one with my preschool son's grinning face framed by dry macaroni painted gold. The gifts from various parishioners from various churches in various states. And the paper cranes that symbolize our hope that God's peace will one day reign over creation.

I spot my daughter's "first Christmas" ornament which is, oddly enough, a tabby-colored kitten in a purple and green baby stroller. And instantly, I remember her other firsts: her first smile, her first solid food, her first step, her first day of school, her first lost tooth. But then a wave of melancholy hits because "firsts" hint to "lasts": the last time I fed her, the last time I carried her to bed, the last time I tied her shoes, the last time I washed her hair.

The trouble with being human is that every step toward one thing is a step away from another thing. And in a fallen world, that path necessarily includes loss. Because I also see the heirloom ornaments—the ones from a childhood that will never return and those that remind me of loved ones passed. This mixture of mirth and melancholy, of life and death, may seem out of place in a season that's supposed to be marked by joy. But the older I grow, the more I realize that Christmas is exactly the time for the bittersweet. And the older I grow, the more I understand why the magi's gift of myrrh is so fitting.

Like frankincense, myrrh is a resin with antimicrobial and healing properties. Collected from a thorny tree of the Commiphora genus, it, too, hardens into solid droplets. So pleasant is myrrh's scent, that despite having multiple applications, it was most often used in perfumes and incense. In fact, myrrh was also one of the main ingredients in the holy anointing oil. The book of Esther mentions her receiving "beauty treatments with oil of myrrh";[1] and Song of Songs repeatedly alludes to its aromatic and erotic properties, describing the lovers as "scented with myrrh" and "dripping with flowing myrrh."[2]

But myrrh's earthy associations with the body extend beyond life into death. The word itself means "bitter," leading some to suggest that the name originated from its use in funeral rites. The ancient Egyptians included myrrh in their mummification process, and by the first century, it was well-established as part of funeral rites.[3] So if gold and frankincense allude to the Promised Son's kingly and priestly roles, myrrh speaks of his coming death.

And here, we must pause. So far, I've asked you to entertain the scandal that God, who created the universe, entered his creation as a baby. I've asked you to consider what it means for the Promised Son to take on flesh, to limit himself to time and space, to carry our brokenness within his own body. But as shocking as it is to consider the birth of God, there's something even more unsettling in considering his death. *That the One who came into the world through Mary's womb would exit it though crucifixion. That the One wrapped in swaddling clothes and laid in a manger would be wrapped in grave clothes and laid in a tomb.* This is holy ground.

But becoming human in a world that groans under the curse means that every first leads to a last. Every step away from the manger is a step toward the cross. And the death of the Promised Son is as certain as his birth.

During his earthly ministry, Jesus speaks often of his coming death. When Mary of Bethany anoints his feet with perfume, he says that she "anointed my body in advance for burial."[4] Traveling up to Jerusalem, he warns his disciples that he "will be handed over to the chief priests and scribes, and they will condemn him to death."[5] So when his hour finally comes, death itself is no surprise. The One who was born in human flesh must now die in the same. And what follows is no surprise either because just like our bodies, the Promised Son's body immediately begins to decompose, breaking down to return to the dust from which it was taken.

Loving him the way they do, Jesus's friends take his mangled corpse and prepare it for burial. Nicodemus—that curious disciple who could not wrap his mind around the new birth but seems to understand the realities of death—brings "a mixture of about seventy-five pounds of myrrh and aloes." Then he and Joseph of Arimathea and the women wrap Jesus's body in linen cloths with the fragrant spices and lay it in a tomb.[6]

Here's the interesting thing about embalming: embalming a dead body is a way to honor it, to show that even in death our bodies are worth expense and devotion. It allows loved ones to offer one final act of care and attention. But the point of embalming, the point of protecting human bodies from decomposition, was to preserve them for the life to come. And so myrrh points not only to death but also to life after death.

Because as much as Jesus spoke of his death, he also spoke of his resurrection. He tells his disciples that he will be killed but also that "on the third day he will be raised up."[7] (And at Lazarus's tomb, he declares, "I am the resurrection and the life. The one who believes in me, even if he dies, will live."[8]

The One who is born must die, but the One who dies must rise.

I read obituaries and walk beside graves to remind myself that I, too, must die one day. I hope this thought changes how I live. But how do I remind myself that I will live again? This seems to me the more pressing need. Death is all around me; and while we do everything we can to delay it, the inevitable always comes. So, how do I remind myself that death is not the end? And how do I do this in a way that honors both my life today as well as my life to come? How do you live if you know that you will rise again?

But then I remember how Jesus lived, how he lived in the truth of the resurrection before it ever happened. Inviting us into this same way of life, Jesus says, "If anyone wants to follow after me, let him deny himself, take up his cross daily, and follow me. For whoever wants to save his life will lose it, but whoever loses his life because of me will save it. For what does it benefit someone if he gains the whole world, and yet loses or forfeits himself?"[9]

Then I also remember how Jesus spent his life caring for those around him. How he taught with both boldness and compassion. How he fed and healed bodies. How he behaved righteously and obeyed the Father. How he gave himself as a sacrifice for us. How he lived at peace with God, with his calling, and with others. How none of this makes sense to people desperate to save their own lives and happiness at every turn.

In Hebrews 2, the writer speaks of Jesus sharing our human experience even to death "so that through his death he might destroy the one holding the power of death—that is, the devil—and free those who were held in slavery all their lives by the fear of death."[10] And then I understand. Jesus does not free us from death. He frees us from fear. He frees us to live and die at peace as he did. He frees us to sacrifice *despite* the pain.

Because to reach resurrection, you must die. You must walk through the valley. And more than anything, the season of Advent calls us to face this reality, to look death straight in the eye. To understand that the creation is groaning and to allow ourselves to groan with it. To know that life on this earth will strip us of all we hold dear and send us back to the ground from which we came.

But this season also teaches us how to make peace with this reality. We may not be able to avoid suffering, but God will hold us safe in the midst of it. So when death comes to us in a hundred different ways, we will trust the One who walked through death to resurrection. We will trust him to carry us through to new life as well.

And so the firsts and the lasts find themselves swallowed up in the forevers. Whatever we grieve today, whatever death takes from us, we cling to the promise that one day it will be no more. We cling to the hope that, though we die, we will live, and one day we will be swallowed up in the life of God himself. And in this hope we find ourselves at peace.

# 24

# Dream State

It's my experience that nobody sleeps well on Christmas Eve, despite the famous line about children being "nestled all snug in the beds/While visions of sugar-plums danced in their heads."[1]

My youngest son, our predictably good sleeper, can never seem to calm himself. He'll start by going to bed a bit early, in the hopes that sleeping will make the time pass more quickly. But within forty-five minutes, he'll wander out of his bedroom again. We'll make a cup of chamomile tea with honey, and he'll try again. An hour later he's still wide-eyed, so I suggest reading. Eventually, I'll consent to a small dose of melatonin to nudge his body to initiate a sleep cycle, but even once he falls asleep, he's still restless. I can tell he's dreaming by the way he mumbles quietly to himself and tosses his hands ever so slightly, but it's not a contented dream. Days of sugary indulgence, disrupted routines, and heightened expectations come to bear in this moment so that even in sleep, he seems exhausted. His sleep is fitful, and he struggles to be at peace.

Given all that has happened in the nativity story to this point, with all the excitement of a new Baby and visits from strangers, I'm not surprised to find interrupted sleep and dreams as part of its conclusion. After presenting their gifts, the magi are "warned in a dream not to go back to Herod."[2]

Scientifically speaking, dreams are a collection of involuntary experiences—emotions, ideas, sensations, and images—that occur while we sleep. They happen in the rapid eye movement (REM) portion of our sleep cycle when our bodies are immobilized but our brain activity most closely corresponds to our waking hours. According to scientists' observations, we spend up to two hours dreaming each night with each dream lasting anywhere from ten to forty-five minutes.

Obviously, it's one thing to dream and another thing to remember our dreams after we wake up. Sometimes we have lucid dreams in which we are actively conscience of dreaming, and sometimes we'll be able to catch vague remnants of dreams, but it's suggested that nearly 95 percent of our dreams are forgotten. This makes it especially difficult to study dreams. Researchers can observe us as we dream and record the frequency, duration, and physical responses that dreams elicit. They can take testimony of how the dreamer experienced and remembered the details of her dream. But because dreams are happening within the mind of the dreamer, they have to rely on her ability to translate what she perceived inside her head.

So just as the world around us pulsates with realities beyond our current reach—with germs and angels alike—dreams occur just beyond the reach of our ability to prove exactly what they are or why they exist. This lack of certainty can be unnerving for a culture taught to rely on external stimuli and cognition to establish reality. But I suppose that's why I appreciate the Bible's matter-of-fact tone toward both dreams and the bodies of those who dream.

In much the same way that Scripture validates human sexuality and other physical experiences, it validates those things that happen beyond our senses. Simply put, the authors of Scripture do not feel the need to explain the presence of dreams in human experience. And in response to the question of whether a dream is a physical phenomenon or a metaphysical one, the Scripture answers with a resounding yes! So when the magi, those men of both science and faith, receive a dream from God that warns them to return home another way, they do.

But the magi's dream is not the only dream Matthew records. Joseph also receives a second dream in which the angel of the Lord comes to him with great urgency, saying, "Get up! Take the child and his mother, flee to Egypt, and stay there until I tell you. For Herod is about to search for the child to kill him."[3]

The next section is one of the darkest of Scripture, especially when laid against the light and joy that precede it. Because just as my son tosses and turns on a night that should be full of wonder, an ancient threat arises in the middle of celebrating the Promised Son—the threat of evil that knows it has been defeated. When the magi do not return to Jerusalem and Herod realizes he has been outplayed, he flies into a rage. He orders all the boys of Bethlehem, two-years-old and under, to be massacred. His soldiers descend on the tiny town and move from house to house, slaughtering with unflinching cruelty, and the nightmare Jeremiah 31 predicted comes true.

> A voice was heard in Ramah,
> a lament with bitter weeping—
> Rachel weeping for her children,
> refusing to be comforted for her children
> because they are no more.[4]

This is also a difficult passage because we know these innocents were only killed because of their proximity to the Promised Son. They were only targeted because Herod was after the infant Jesus. But because of divine intervention, Joseph, Mary, and the Baby escape to Egypt. And if I'm honest, it all feels so senseless. *Why all the pointless suffering? Why all the meaningless devastation? Why did so many people have to* be harmed? *If the Promised Son is safe, why did these other sons have to die?*

But then I remember: the cruelty is the point.

Slaughtering innocents en masse has never been a reasonable response. Not when Pharaoh did it in Egypt. Not when Herod did it in Bethlehem. Not when dictators do it today. These are not the sensible actions of a ruler protecting his rule. They are the rage and insecurity of one who's realized he is powerless.

Speaking allegorically, Revelation 12 reveals that this kind of senseless destruction is exactly how the evil one responds when he understands that he cannot stop God's plan:

> When the dragon saw that he had been thrown down to the earth, he persecuted the woman who had given birth to the male child. . . . So the dragon was furious with the woman and went off to wage war against the rest of her offspring—those who keep the commands of God and hold firmly to the testimony about Jesus.[5]

Such violence seems senseless precisely because it is. It is the rage of the old serpent, writhing and coiling under the foot of the Promised Son. The serpent has been crushed, but with his last bit of strength, he lunges at those the Father loves. And just as an animal is most dangerous when it is wounded, there is none so dangerous as the old serpent who knows he is dying.

But even in this, the Promised Son does not abandon us. Because eventually, Jesus will himself carry the full force of evil on the cross, and when his body lies for three nights in the tomb, wrapped in myrrh and spices, immobilized in the sleep of death, he will break the power hell holds over the world. He will end the nightmare.

Eventually Herod dies just as evil one day must. And the Lord appears to Joseph again, but this time it is with good news. In the same Scripture that prophesies the senseless evil that steals away Rachel's children, the Lord says,

> Keep your voice from weeping
> and your eyes from tears,
> for the reward for your work will come—
> this is the LORD's declaration—
> and your children will return from the
>     enemy's land.
> There is hope for your future—
> this is the LORD's declaration—
> and your children will return.[6]

As the story ends, God calls the Promised Son home from afar, and the words of Psalm 30 ring true:

> LORD, you brought me up from Sheol;
> you spared me from among those
> going down to the Pit. . . .
> Weeping may stay overnight,
> but there is joy in the morning.[7]

Through the season of Advent, we learn to mourn all that is broken in the world. As we begin to understand the depth of evil, as the shadows gather round us, it can feel like we are descending into the gloom, never to return. We're desperate to be free of our restless dreams. But here in the night, in the waiting and the longing, when even our sleep haunts us, we know that morning will come, just as he has promised. Morning will come; we will awaken safe in his arms. And try as they might, all the forces of hell are powerless to stop it.

# 25

# Christmas Morn

**M**orning has finally come.

Nathan and I get to sleep in these days, but when the children were younger, celebrations began in the predawn hours. With one caveat. Growing up, Nathan's side of the family always sat down to breakfast before opening gifts, and it's something he's continued—to the consistent protest of our children. (It's possible that I've sided with them on more than one occasion over the years.) But since it's important to him, I've learned to have breakfast ready as quickly and as simply as possible. For us, that means a pan of tempting sweet rolls, scrambled or boiled eggs, and orange juice.

A rabbi once told me that the most neglected piece of religious furniture is the family table and that the surest way to guarantee your children will not continue in faith is to neglect habits of faith at home. But he also told me that one of the simplest ways to prioritize faith at home is to give children a fully embodied experience of it. They need to breathe in seasonal scents, to taste the sweetness of holiday foods, to be part of preparing them, to decorate the house and buy gifts and celebrate holy days until they learn these rhythms by heart. All while we teach them what makes these days holy in the first place.

And so I now understand "Christmas is for children" slightly differently than I used to. When people say such things, they often mean that Christmas is magical and playful—that, in their naiveté, children experience the holiday differently than adults. While we drag ourselves out of bed and insist on breakfast, they jump and run and cannot wait for the celebration to begin. And so it's our responsibility, they say, to put all our energy and attention into giving children the most exciting, memorable day possible.

But I wonder if "Christmas is for children" really speaks to the way quieter traditions shape us, how years of sitting down to breakfast before unwrapping presents gains a kind of momentum that carries itself forward into life. I also wonder whether "Christmas is for children" testifies to the reason we are celebrating in the first place. Because while Advent reminds us of why we long for the Promised Son, Christmas delivers him to us as a baby.

On this morning, as we celebrate the One who will restore peace to the world, we must also attend to the fact that he came to us as a child. That all he promises us is somehow tied to this reality. In Isaiah 11, the prophet offers us a vision of what creation at rest might look like, and right in the middle of it all, is a child.

> The wolf will dwell with the lamb,
> and the leopard will lie down with the goat.
> The calf, the young lion, and the fattened
> calf will be together,
> and a child will lead them . . .
>
> On that day the root of Jesse
> will stand as a banner for the peoples.
> The nations will look to him for guidance,
> and his resting place will be glorious.[1]

There's a particularly famous painting of this vision done by Edward Hicks, a carriage painter turned preacher turned artist. If you ever find yourself in the National Gallery in Washington, D.C., head to the West Building and

Gallery 63. There among other early American artists, you'll find *Peaceable Kingdom of the Branch*, Hicks's portrayal of wild beasts lying at peace with their natural enemies. The colors are muted and the varnish cracked, and yet Hicks's primitive style somehow lends a childlike aura to the scene.

But you can also find a similar painting in the Metropolitan Museum of Art in New York City. Another in the Philadelphia Museum of Art. And one each in the Brooklyn Museum of Art; the Reynolda House Museum of American Art in Winston-Salem, North Carolina; and the De Young Museum in San Francisco. Because over the course of forty years, Hicks painted this scene from Isaiah 11 at least sixty-two times.

Each version varies in setting and background elements, but the core imagery remains the same: a collection of beasts—a lion, leopard, bear, and calf—sit patiently together, and among them children play. And one child, the Christ child, always holds a branch in his curled fist—the shoot from the root of Jesse. Curators note that Hicks's attention to Isaiah 11 grew out of his religious devotion, but this doesn't explain the sheer number of paintings. *What could inspire a man to paint the same scene over and over again? What could make him devote forty years of his life to one chapter of the Bible?*

I suppose it could be religious commitment, but I wonder if it wasn't also longing. The longing for war to cease. The longing for all things to be made right. The longing for the world to be at peace. Indeed, so deep is our longing for peace that we often settle for substitutes. We opt for the enforced peace of a *Pax Romana* where the strength of the government keeps everyone in line. Or we settle for tolerance that, more often than not, is just distance and condescension. We ignore wrongdoing in order to avoid conflict. And within our own hearts, we make all kinds of bargains to avoid the truth that leads to shalom.

But the peace of God is not peace as we understand it. It is not a peace that acquiesces. It is not a peace that coerces or condescends. It is a peace so strong, so stable, so elemental that he can send a child to initiate it.

So it's no coincidence that Isaiah's vision of the peaceable kingdom includes children. It's no coincidence that only two chapters earlier, he foretells the coming of the Promised Son with these words:

> For unto us a child is born, unto us a son
> is given: and the government shall be upon
> his shoulder: and his name shall be called
> Wonderful, Counsellor, The mighty God,
> The everlasting Father, The Prince of Peace.[2]

And now I understand why someone would paint that vision over and over again. I understand how each rendering, each new canvas, each brush stroke could both assuage and intensify the longing for God's peace to reign.

Because every year, we do the same on Christmas morning.

Every year, as we celebrate the birth of the Prince of peace, we rehearse and retell our own longing for God's shalom. Through our decorations, holiday food, church services, wrapped gifts, and joyful songs, we teach one another to believe in the hope of the Promised Son. A hope the apostle Paul describes this way in Colossians 1:

> He is the image of the invisible God,
> the firstborn over all creation.
> For everything was created by him,
> in heaven and on earth,
> the visible and the invisible,
> whether thrones or dominions
> or rulers or authorities—

all things have been created through him
    and for him.
He is before all things,
and by him all things hold together.
He is also the head of the body, the church;
he is the beginning,
the firstborn from the dead,
so that he might come to have
first place in everything.
For God was pleased to have
all his fullness dwell in him,
and through him to reconcile
everything to himself,
whether things on earth or things in heaven,
by making peace
through his blood, shed on the cross.[3]

And so with heaven and nature, we sing. We sing in praise, and we sing in sorrow. We sing in hope, and we sing in faith, longing for the peace that all of us—that beast and bird and sky and hill and body and mind—desperately crave. We sing in praise of our infant Creator King, who by coming to us as a child, teaches us how to come to him.

"Let the little children come to me," Jesus says. "Don't stop them, because the kingdom of God belongs to such as these."[4] And again: "Truly I tell you, unless you turn and become like little children, you will never enter the kingdom of heaven. Therefore, whoever humbles himself like this child—this one is the greatest in the kingdom of heaven."[5] The story of Advent and Christmas is the rehearsing of these truths over and over again. It is the story of a creation groaning, longing to be reconciled to its Creator. It is the story of a Promised Son come as a Baby. It is a story of sacrifice and redemption, of not just new life but life after death. And it is a story we must keep telling and retelling until it is finally and fully true, both within our own hearts and in the world around us. This is how the kingdom comes. And this is how we enter it.

# About the Author and Illustrator

**Hannah Anderson** is an author and Bible teacher who lives in the Blue Ridge Mountains of Virginia with her husband, Nathan, and their three children. Her books include *All That's Good: Recovering the Lost Art of Discernment* and *Turning of Days: Lessons from Nature, Season, and Spirit.* She also cohosts the Persuasion podcast, which addresses cultural, theological, and more mundane issues from a Christian perspective. Hannah's goal is to encourage believers to think deeply and broadly about how the gospel transforms every area of life.

**Nathan Anderson** is an illustrator and ordained minister who holds master's degrees in theology and leadership. A native of southwest Virginia, he is most at home walking in the woods, working in his garden, or birding with the Roanoke Valley Bird Club. You can find more of his work on Instagram at @nathan_d_anderson.

# Acknowledgments

Just as the holidays are meant to be shared in community, this book would not exist apart from the people who surround us with love and support, including:

The team at B&H—not the least, Ashley, Jade, and Susan. Many thanks for your work and vision. You made the process seamless and enjoyable. No small feat!

Erik W., partner in this work of writing.

All our friends who remember to send us holiday cards even when we don't remember to send them in return.

The churches that have sheltered us through our family's life together, carrying forward our common faith through Christmas pageants, dinners, caroling, gift exchanges, cantatas, candlelit services, and most importantly, bags of homemade candy and cookies.

Our extended families, with whom we've shared so many Christmas hams and turkeys.

Our parents, Phillip and Lydia Strickler and Dennis and Judy Anderson, who spent years establishing the traditions that we carry with us to this day.

Phoebe, Harry, and Peter, who make our Christmases past, present, and future so full of meaning and wonder.

And finally, Francis and Ben, who teach us more about our Infant Creator than they may ever know.

# Notes

### 1. Wintering

1. Romans 8:19–21.
2. Genesis 3:19. This is a phrase found in many Christian events (funerals, etc.), and is commonly used as a way to harken to this verse.
3. "Joy to the World," lyrics by Isaac Watts (1719), public domain.

### 2. The Serpent

1. Genesis 3:14–15.
2. Romans 3:12–13.
3. John 3:14–16.
4. "Joy to the World," lyrics by Isaac Watts (1719), public domain.

### 3. Family Tree

1. Isaiah 10:33.
2. Isaiah 6:13.
3. Isaiah 11:1–2, 10.

### 4. Anointed One

1. Elizabeth Barrett Browning, "Aurora Leigh."
2. Exodus 30:34–38.

3. Though this phrase is somewhat common in certain religious and philosophical circles, definite attribution is difficult to cite. Most attribute this phrase to Saint Augustine.

4. John 10:22.

5. Isaiah 53:5.

## 5. Silence

1. "The Science behind Snow's Serenity," Science Daily, January 21, 2016, https://www.sciencedaily.com/releases/2016/01/160121150503.htm.

2. "The End of Prophecy: Malachi's Position in the Spiritual Development of Israel," Ideals, accessed February 27, 2022, https://www.jewishideas.org/article/end-prophecy-malachis-position-spiritual-development-israel.

3. Malachi 4:5–6.

4. Luke 1:18.

5. Luke 1:19–20.

6. Luke 1:13.

7. Genesis 1:3.

8. I Samuel 1:13.

9. Isaiah 65:24.

10. Romans 8:26–27.

11. Hebrews 1:1–2.

## 6. Holy Seed

1. Psalm 139:13–15.

2. Luke 1:31–32.

3. Luke 1:35.

4. Luke 1:38.

5. James 1:18.

6. James 1:21–22.

7. 1 John 3:1–3 HCSB.

8. Luke 18:27.

## 7. Every Valley

1. Genesis 7:11 KJV.

2. Luke 1:39, emphasis added.

3. Luke 1:15.

4. Isaiah 40:3–5.

5. Luke 1:46–48, 51–52 KJV.

6. Psalm 147:6 ESV.

7. Luke 1:76–79.

8. Isaiah 60:1 KJV.

## 8. Family Land

1. Luke 1:32.

2. Luke 3:23.

3. Romans 8:31–32, 35, 38–39.

## 9. Birth Pains

1. Genesis 3:16 KJV.

2. Revelation 12:3–4.

3. Luke 1:38 HCSB.

4. Genesis 35:16, 19–20.

5. 1 Timothy 2:14–15.

6. Galatians 4:4–5.

7. John 16:20–21.

8. 1 Peter 1:5–7.

## 10. Evergreen

1. Henry van Dyke, "The First Christmas Tree," https://americanliterature.com/author/henry-van-dyke/short-story/the-first-christmas-tree.

2. van Dyke, "The First Christmas Tree."

3. Exodus 22:29–30; Numbers 14–16.

4. Luke 2:7 KJV.

5. Hebrews 13:8.

6. This is the 1975 ecumenical translation of the Nicene Creed as seen in many denominational settings, songbooks, and prayer guides, one of which can be found in *The Book of Common Prayer* (New York: Church Hymnal Corporation, 1979), 358–59.

7. Romans 8:29 KJV.

8. Hebrews 1:3.

## 11. Swaddling Bands

1. Luke 2:7.

2. *De Sanitate Tuenda*, in T. E. C. Jr., "Galen on the Hygiene of the Newborn," *Pediatrics*, https://publications.aap.org/pediatrics/article-abstract/52/6/840/45146/GALEN-ON-THE-HYGIENE-OF-THE-NEWBORN?redirectedFrom=fulltext.

3. Genesis 3:21.

4. Isaiah 49:15.

5. Isaiah 66:13.

6. Matthew 6:28, 30.

7. John 20:7.

8. Revelation 7:9.

## 12. No Room

1. Luke 2:7.

2. John 1:10–11.

3. Matthew 8:19–20.

4. John 14:23.

5. John 14:1–3.

## 13. Among the Beasts

1. Genesis 2:19–20.

2. Romans 5:15, 20.

3. "Joy to the World," lyrics by Isaac Watts (1719), public domain.

4. Psalm 104:24, 27–28.

5. Matthew 6:26.

6. Matthew 6:31–33.

## 14. Keeping Watch

1. 1 Samuel 16:11; 17:34.

2. Psalm 121:1.

3. Psalm 121:2–8.

4. Hebrews 6:10.

5. Luke 2:10.

6. 1 Corinthians 15:58.

7. Isaiah 65:25.

## 15. The Good Shepherd

1 Luke 2:10–11.

2. Micah 5:2–4.

3. John 10:14–16.

4. Proverbs 29:2 NKJV.

5. Jeremiah 23:1–2.

6. Jeremiah 23:4.

7. Jeremiah 23:5–6.

## 16. Visible and Invisible

1. Luke 2:9–14.

2. Colossians 2:18.

3. Luke 2:15.

4. Hebrews 1:6–7.

## 17. Birds and Bees

1. Luke 2:22–24.

2. Genesis 17:10–14.

3. Leviticus 12:4.

4. Leviticus 12:6–8.

5. Matthew 21:12.

6. 1 Corinthians 6:11, 19.

## 18. Boughs of Holly

1. Mark Cartwright, "A Medieval Christmas," *World History Encyclopedia*, December 1, 2018, https://www.worldhistory.org/article/1288/a-medieval-christmas.

2. Luke 2:25.

3. Luke 2:39.

4. Luke 2:29–32.

5. Luke 2:34–35.

6. 1 Peter 4:12–13.

## 19. Fullness of Time

1. Luke 2:38.
2. Luke 2:36.
3. 2 Peter 1:19–21.
4. 2 Peter 1:19.
5. Hebrews 11:13.
6. 2 Peter 1:15.
7. Hebrews 11:39–12:2.
8. Psalm 71:18.

## 20. Starry Night

1. "More Meteors Streak through Moonless Midnights, Winter Is Coming!," Star Walk, December 18, 2017, https://starwalk.medium.com/more-meteors-streak-through-moonless-midnights-winter-is-coming-bd576ee4164c.
2. Psalm 19:1.
3. Matthew 2:1.
4. J Gresham Machen, *The Virgin Birth of Christ* (James Clarke & Co, 1958), 197.
5. Matthew 2:1–2.
6. Greg Cootona, "What Kind of Astronomical Marvel was the Star of Bethlehem?," *Christianity Today*, November 23, 2015, https://www.christianitytoday.com/ct/2015/december/what-kind-of-astronomical-marvel-was-star-of-bethlehem.html.
7. Isaiah 60:1–4.
8. John 14:6.
9. Luke 13:28–29.
10. Daniel 12:3.

## 21. Gold

1. Matthew 2:2 NET.
2. Isaiah 60:3, 5–6.
3. Matthew 28:18–19.

4. Matthew 2:3.

5. Philippians 2:10–11.

6. Revelation 21:21, 23–24, 26.

## 22. Frankincense

1. Revelation 18:12–13.

2. Matthew 24:2.

3. Luke 2:49.

4. Mark 11:17.

5. Isaiah 56:6–7.

6. 1 Timothy 2:1–6.

7. Revelation 21:22–24.

## 23. Myrrh

1. Esther 2:12.

2. Song of Songs 3:6; 5:13.

3. https://www.ncbi.nlm.nih.gov/pmc/articles/PMC3931544/

4. Mark 14:8.

5. Matthew 20:18.

6. John 19:38–42.

7. Matthew 17:23.

8. John 11:25.

9. Luke 9:23–25.

10. Hebrews 2:14–15.

## 24. Dream State

1. The 1823 Christmas poem "The Night before Christmas" by Clement Clarke Moore.

2. Matthew 2:12.

3. Matthew 2:13.

4. Jeremiah 31:15.

5. Revelation 12:13, 17.

6. Jeremiah 31:16–17.

7. Psalm 30:3, 5.

## 25. Christmas Morn

1. Isaiah 11:6, 10.
2. Isaiah 9:6 KJV.
3. Colossians 1:15–20.
4. Mark 10:14.
5. Matthew 18:3–4.